MW00325786

The Q.U.E.E.N Xperience Guide to Playing Your Royal Position II

SNATCH YOUR CONFIDENCE BACK!

Visionary Author: Min. Nakita Davis

A Queen Collaborative Book

Unless otherwise indicated, all Scripture quotations are taken from the HOLY BIBLE, NEW INTERNATIONAL VERSION®. NIV®. Copyright © 1973, 1978, 1984 by International Bible Society. Used by permission of Zondervan. All rights reserved worldwide. All Scripture quotations marked NKJV are taken from the New King James Version®. Copyright © 1982 by Thomas Nelson. Used by permission. All rights reserved.

For permission requests, write to the publisher, addressed "Attention: Permissions Coordinator," at the address: 1700 Northside Dr. Suite A7-5055, Atlanta, GA 30318.

Presenting Author: Min. Nakita Davis – Publishing House Publisher: Jesus, Coffee, and Prayer Christian Publishing 1700 Northside Dr. Suite A7-5055, Atlanta, GA 30318; www.jesuscoffeeandprayer.com – Cover: Chief Editor: Jesus, Coffee, and Prayer Christian Publishing House LLC

Paperback ISBN 978-1-952273-16-2

TABLE OF CONTENTS

DEDICATION

This book is dedicated to All My Queens who have
DROPPED the excuses, REFUSED to lose, and are READY
to Play Their Royal Position!

I See You, Queen

Keep WINNING for His Glory!

Min. Nakita Davis

A NOTE FROM THE PUBLISHER
OF PURPOSE

This year has been one for the books~ no pun intended.

There were all-time lows experienced and felt by many and enormous highs that only the Good Lord could bring with breakthrough!

No matter if you were on the short end of the stick or experienced supernatural favor; know that each season, each obstacle, each victory has built you and shaped you for a time such as this!

In this hour, pray for wisdom, discernment, and the kind of authentic relationships that will last a lifetime!

Your Greater is on the other side of your obedience, your calling, and YOU NEVER GIVING UP!

Queen, It's Time to Play Your Royal Position!

PLAY YOUR POSITION AS A QUEEN. KNOW YOUR WORTH AND UNDERSTAND WHO YOU ARE!

TINA RAMSAY

1 Thessalonians 5:17

Pray continually, (NIV)

Philippians 4:13

I can do all this through him who gives me strength (NIV)

Do you truly understand who a Queen is? Let me feel you in on something: You don't need to have a King; be the ruler of a country; imagine yourself as a Disney Fairy Tale Character; or be rich to be a Queen. A Queen is any woman, regardless of her background or education. A Queen is not defined by her past, but how she overcomes and moves on. A Queen is you and your ability to see and believe yourself as such; a mindset of self-love, growth, and self-worth.

When someone called me a Queen in the past, I felt very uncomfortable because I felt unworthy of that title. However, now, I know that I deserve that title. That's not arrogance; it's knowing your worth and embracing it. **ALL WOMEN ARE QUEENS,** not just me. So, in order for you to take your position, you first have to know your value. This starts with you developing the proper mindset about yourself. I am Tina Ramsay, your Certified Development Coach, Author, International Public Speaker, Influential Women Who Win, Diamond Menstrual Health Advocate, Community Volunteer, Natural Wellness Educator, Girl Scouts of America Community Partner, and the CEO/Founder of HealTheHoneypot.com, and **I AM A QUEEN!**

Did you know that the Queen is the most powerful piece on the chessboard? But why? The Queen is the only piece on the board that has the ability to move on any number of squares, vertical, horizontal, and diagonal. Understand your strength, Queens, especially when the storms come. This will help you to push through anything by learning how to pivot your business and life when necessary to make continued progress.

So, does having the mindset of a Queen alleviate or shield you from problems, adversity, and challenges in life or your business? No, it does not. On the contrary, as you build and grow your business, you will face all the above and more. But, when these problems arise, do you allow them to shift or remove your crown?

Queens, I want you to understand that **Adversity**, **Failure**, **Headaches,** goes with the territory of business. One of my favorite quotes is by Napoleon Hill, which says: "Every adversity, every failure, every heartache carries with it the seed of an equal or greater benefit." As a Business Owner, you need to develop that "I Can Do" mindset, even when you feel like you can't. Problems can actually be a blessing, in the sense that they can teach you endurance, patience, insight, and the quality to push through to achieve your breakthrough. How? **PROBLEMS** have the **ABILITY** to **LEAD** you to Your **SOLUTION**, then that Solution **POSITIONS** you to make an **IMPACT** in the **WORLD**, by you sharing your **WISDOM** and **JUST TELLING YOUR STORY**. Your *Knowledge*, Your *Resilience*, Your *Endurance*, can *Empower* other women (Queens) all over the world.

Problems and challenges teach us to persevere, endure, and **rely on God** to pull us through by having faith in Him.

A Queen accepts her assignment, even if she doesn't understand everything. (This Takes Faith.) Hebrews 11:1

Now faith is confidence in what we hope for and assurance about what we do not see. (NIV)

When You Are on the Wrong Assignment.

I was on the wrong assignment for most of my life. The right title, but wrong purpose. All of my life, I always knew that I wanted to be a teacher. My passion was to not only be a teacher, but also a voice for the voiceless. So I worked with Behavioral Problem Students and Special Needs Children. Also, I tutored children in underprivileged neighborhoods being their advocate. I was very good at what I did. I loved helping and seeing my students thrive. However, one thing that puzzled me was that although I was a teacher and doing what I said I would do with my life, **I WAS NOT FULFILLED!** I could not understand this. How could this be?

Challenge
1 Peter 5:10

And the God of all grace, who called you to his eternal glory in Christ, after you have suffered a little while, will himself restore you and make you strong, firm, and steadfast. (NIV)

At the age of 25, I had a stroke that left me partially paralyzed from the waist down and I lost my short-term memory. I was a new mother and wife to a beautiful newborn little girl. So, in my youth, the prime of my life, I had to depend on my husband and parents to not only take care of me, but also my newborn baby. This was very difficult for me and I fell into a deep dark depression. I prayed a lot, even though I personally felt that God had forgotten me or that I must have done something wrong. I was like, "Why me?" I felt trapped within my own body. Young by age, but my body and my health were that of an unhealthy senior citizen. Taking 12 medications and 4 inhalers a day. I could not understand this because all my life I always ate right and exercised regularly, never smoked. Why was this happening to me? I followed the Bible and did my best to follow Jesus' fine example. I was just at a loss for words. I was heartbroken and felt completely alone. But with all that, I never stopped praying.

Then, one day, my epiphany moment came. I always watched my food, diet, and exercise, but I never watched the medicines and products that I used in my home for cleaning, or products that I used in and on my body. I started doing research and making changes. Over time, I regained my short-term memory back and my ability to walk. I am no longer on 12 medication or 4 inhalers.

I shared my story to help people wanting to start their wellness journey naturally. I've helped so many individuals start their Natural Wellness Journey inspiring them through my life.

The Problem I Hid for 25 years

I was suffering in silence for 25 years. I went to doctors, took tests, and everything came back normal. No matter what I did, I could not figure out how to solve this problem completely, even with Natural Remedies. I felt like a fraud. Here I was, a Natural Wellness Coach, and this one last thing I could not solve, even with my best effort.

This problem was so bad that when I found out that I was pregnant, I prayed to God not to have a girl.

So, what was this problem that I hid that made me feel like a fraud? I had terrible cycles. I am talking about the kind of period that you miss work, school, trips, and outings because you are just too sick and weak to go. The kind of period that puts you in depression mode each and every month for 25 years. I prayed for the wisdom to solve this problem so that I could help my daughter whose period was worse than mine. I refused to allow her suffer like me for 25 years. There had to be another way. So, I kept on praying.

Then, one night, my husband woke me up and showed me a video that changed my life. Then, from that video, we went to a conference to learn more. At that conference, I got the products and my life has never been the same again. I got my **BREAKTHROUGH!** I no longer suffer in silence and I have the knowledge to help women and girls to stop period suffering. I explain how most Pads and Tampons out today are loaded with toxic chemicals which can affect your health, your period, and mental wellbeing.

Finding the solution to my problem birthed my business and it's how I found my passion, joy, and being fulfilled. God has positioned me **To Give Females the Best Cycle Experience Ever!** He's enabled me to help females heal their mind, body, and honeypots naturally and avoid the 25 years of suffering I had to endure.

God has a Sense of Humor
Accepting Your Assignment: Pandemic: The Pivot

I never thought in a million years that I would be *teaching about Menstrual Health & Mindset Development*. I absolutely love what I do. I am finally **FULFILLED**. When I decided to accept my assignment, things started to change for the better, but not without challenges. I had to start pivoting my business from totally in-person to be online because of the Pandemic. Queens, I had to network, support, and **lock arms with the right Queens** to grow my business and influence. I had to pray, be consistent, ask for help, learn, and invest in my business.

I am still on this journey of growth. 2020 has taught me to follow through on the assignment assigned to me, even if I don't completely understand it. (Takes Faith and Trust.) I have had successes, failures, adversities, and joys all in 2020. This Pandemic has taught me **complete reliance on God, to trust His process designed for me**.

Consistent Growth Despite the Pandemic

By **allowing God to direct my steps,** my business has grown and given birth to a new horizon. This adjustment was not easy for me to trust and walk into. I trusted God and let go for this change to take place. This change will allow me to level up my business despite this Pandemic. It takes Faith to follow through on the unknown. Queens, it's your season to win. Trust the process, follow through, continue to pivot, and always allow God to direct your steps (Jer 10:23).

I prayed for God to refine my Direction/Business/Life, and this was my answer: *TINA, YOU ARE THE BRAND!* I am leading my thriving Heal The Honeypot Business now as **Coach Tina Ramsay**. This change was not easy! My HTH Business started the foundation for me to find myself. I had to grow into being secure enough to lead with myself and not my brand. This pandemic has prepared me to walk truly in my Queenhood of acceptance and knowing that I am truly enough. My Heal The Honeypot brand is a wonderful extension of me, but **I am Tina Ramsay, your Certified Development Coach**.

My seeds of adversity have grown towards the greater benefit. Before the Pandemic, I had only one main product, our Reign (Jewel) Premium Sanitary Napkins. However, now, we have Coaching Services, Classes, HTH Organic V-Steams, Essential Oils, Soaps, Natural Candles, Mindset Pocket Journal, Wellness Bundle Boxes, Podcast and Heal The Honeypot TV Show with advertisement opportunities for you to promote your business with us. There are no limits to your growth when you allow God to truly navigate your Life and continue to seek first the Kingdom (Matthew 6:33).

About the Author:

Tina Ramsay is a Certified Development Coach, International Public Speaker, Diamond Menstrual Health Advocate, Author, Community Volunteer, Girl Scouts of America Community Partner, Influential Women Who Wins Honoree, Ambassador /Volunteer for SHE Trucking Community, and Founder/CEO of HealTheHoneypot.com.

She's a force to be reckoned with, because of her collaborations within the wellness and coaching industry with partnerships and natural product suppliers. She places their products/services under her Heal The Honeypot brand umbrella becoming your go-to Wellness Hub for Natural Products & Services.

Stay Connected with this Queen:

Coach Tina Ramsay, CEO of Heal The Honeypot

Website: https://www.healthehoneypot.com/

FB: Facebook.com/HealTheHoneypot & CoachTinaRamsay

IG: Instagram.com/heal_the_honeypot & CoachTinaRamsay

YT: Heal The Honeypot

Email: coachtinaramsay@gmail.com

SNATCHED!
THE POWER OF BREAKING FREE
FROM EXCUSES

CHARCORA PALMER, MBA

"And from the days of John the Baptist until now the kingdom suffereth violence, and the violent take it by force." - Matthew 11:12

The Prelude

Let's face it; everyone has a dream, but sometimes life's circumstances distract us from the promises of God or sometimes, we even get in our own way. I get it! I do, because it happened to me, several times, actually. Oh, but the power of examining where you are and God's promises for you will free your mind and life. Queen, it's time to get SNATCHED! Snatch back your mind. Snatch back your power. Snatch back your promise!

My Journey

One's path is not always charted clearly. I mean, I always knew that my life was destined for greatness; I just didn't know in what capacity the promise would be fulfilled. I started off in the traditional way of going to school, getting good grades, and going off to college. I was proud of myself and so was my family, but that didn't last long. After about a year and a half, I became distracted and college became a thing of the past. I started working in sectors that I never desired myself and then also dibbled and dabbled with network marketing, only to find myself unfulfilled. For a while, I was down on myself because in my eyes, I failed myself and my family. I was supposed to be a doctor, but I got in my own way.

I later returned to college to obtain my undergraduate degree in Business Administration, as my fire for the medical field had died. It was a challenge, as I worked during the day and three times a week in the evening. It was the sacrifice that I had to make at the time, to at least get a degree to have better career opportunities, right? Wow, I was wrong. While I was very elated to obtain my degree and got started in a very rewarding career in the Human Services field, I was yet disappointed. Human Services was not what I attended school for, but I found myself loving the opportunity to serve.

In my mission of serving families in the Human Services field, I became dedicated to assisting them in completely rebuilding their lives after natural disasters. It was then that I noticed my passion for helping others, and I did just that until I found my entire department, including myself, being laid off. I was devastated, as you can imagine. I found myself asking the Lord, "What now?" I found myself relocating back home to Milwaukee to be closer to my family in the time of transition of many levels and continued my Human Services Career with the aim of assisting the elderly and disabled. Again, I fell in love with my occupation because of the opportunity to serve, but it yet was not enough. I had to do something different.

I decided to return to college to obtain my degree in Business Administration so that even if I were to start a business with serving as its focus, I would be able to operate it properly. This time, I was working full-time, married and divorced with two children. I had a goal to reach, but I also wanted to be a mother to my children, so not to impose on anyone else, I opted to go to school online. This required me sacrificing late nights to study after my toddlers were laid down for the evening.

Queen, whatever you put your mind to, you can succeed. Just don't get in your own way. It is easy for life's circumstances to become excuses/crutch, but when you know your purpose, you will lend what it takes to achieve it. Will the road be easy? Absolutely not. Will it be worth it? Of course, it will.

While my Master's Degree did not lend itself to career advancement or life in the corporate sector, it prepared me for my purpose. With my divorce came loss of household income and debt, so I began to examine how to repair my credit and build wealth. I was now solely responsible for two children, and I wanted to provide them the best of life possible while also keeping in mind God's promises over my life. He said in His word that I was the head and not the tail. For me at the time, it didn't add up, as I was experiencing lack. He said that I am the lender and not the borrower, but again, I didn't see that manifestation in my life, as I was trying to find a way to pay off the lenders.

I TOOK IT BY FORCE AND SO CAN YOU.

"And from the days of John the Baptist until now the kingdom suffereth violence, and the violent take it by force - Matthew 11:12.

It was within my personal journey that my passion for helping others was birthed and the calling to help rebuild lives was discovered. While it may have been easier for me to begin to walk in His purpose, without the student loans, late nights as a single parent, loss of a job and a marriage, it was the breaking that anointed what I do. Now, ministering to the financial needs of others is blessed because of my testimony. The journey was challenging and painful, but it was necessary!

My journey has not been a pre-made, scripted template, but one of tests and triumphs. Tears of pain and tears of joy. Discouragement of things not working out in my plan, but encouragement of it working out for my good. Queens, hold on! Whatever is purposed for you will come to pass. Even though I took the long way around, God brought me full circle, and my business became my ministry!

The excuses of it not working out as I planned could have deterred me from by purpose; instead, I decided to embrace the purpose of God and began to walk in His way. I snatched the Key of Faith and it unlocked the door. I refused to doubt God as I know what He spoke over my life. I snatched my mind! Along the journey, I became weary of what seemed to be bad luck happening to me. I went through periods of despair and depression, having seemingly lost all. However, one day, I came to the realization that it was only a trick of the enemy, to deter me from reaching for the promises of God. I made an intentional effort to not focus on what I had lost, but what was to come. I refused to allow the devil to have my mind, as I am a firm believer that if you lose your mind, you lose everything, as the mind is the origin of which everything that makes you human, starts.

I snatched my power. I'm convinced that there is nothing more damaging to a person than to have their power stripped away in whatever capacity one operates. For me, the power of perseverance and confidence were being diminished. There were times in which I was so downtrodden that I didn't have the power to pray and speak life back into myself. I had begun to slowly accept that all was lost and windows of opportunity were closed to me, all while fighting an inward battle of seeing myself through the eyes of a powerful God. In that moment, I made a conscious decision to fight, even when I didn't understand why.

Be encouraged on your journey and snatch back anything the enemy has or is trying to steal from you. Be intentional and everything must come into alignment with what God has purposed for your life. You are worth it, Queen! Don't you dare give up!

About the Author:

The Owner and CEO of Total P.O.W.E.R. Financial Solutions, LLC. Based in Milwaukee, WI, but servicing clients nationwide. Charcora obtained both her Bachelor and Master's degrees in Business Administration. She is nationally certified in the areas of Tax Preparation, Loan Brokerage, and Credit Repair.

Total P.O.W.E.R. Financial Solutions LLC was developed to empower communities through financial education. POWER stands for Positioning Our Wealth for Economic Redevelopment, and with that as a forefront, lives can be forever changed.

Stay Connected with this Queen:

Facebook: @totalpowerfinancial

Instagram: @totalpowerfinancial

LinkedIn: @charcorapalmer

THE GAME CHANGER

AKYA CANADA

To win the game, you first have to get in the game! Don't be afraid to play the game. Be afraid of not believing in yourself enough that you think you don't deserve to be in the game.

Transparent Moment:
Truth is:

I'm scared every day I do something different that challenges me. The stuff I'm doing I've never seen anyone do before.

Have I failed? Yes.

Have I gone broke going after my dreams? Yes.

Have I had to start over? Yes.

I've had to walk away from what I was familiar with into the unknown. But if I say, "I CAN'T LOSE" and God's word says, "He will never leave me or forsake me," I'd be CRAZY if I didn't at least TRY! I always lean on these two scriptures: Jeremiah Ch. 29 v 11 NLT and Habakkuk Ch. 2 v 2-3 NLT to get me through.

***

So it's only been a year since I was let go from my nine-to-five job. Truth be told, I had already been in the planning stages of resigning from the position I held at a very nice upscale salon as a stylist, but fear and doubt paralyzed me. However, to my surprise, God had already strategized my way of escape. When that day came I gave my thank you and said my goodbyes, with such a peace in my spirit I couldn't even describe or explain. November 2019 was when the game changed for me and my life has not been the same!

With no savings in the bank, barely any money in my checking account, just a well-written blueprint of having my own salon and the fire of God pushing me out, I began my entrepreneurial journey. Everyone suggested that I should file for unemployment with the company that let me go, but I said "NO" because I knew God would supply all my needs. Friends told me to file a case, but I said "NO" because "vengeance is mine, says the Lord."

While the plan continued to unfold, I gained temporary employment at my aunt's salon and I gave myself six months to a year to build a strong clientele. While working under her, God began to move in my understanding of business; I gleaned so much from watching and doing; I was coming into my own groove. Or so I thought.

It's funny to me how God will allow you to think you're making moves but all the while He is about to flip the script. Let's just say the open door was abruptly closed at my aunt's salon. Now, I had a deadline of four weeks in counting to find my own salon space. You talking about someone sweating bullets and trying not to break down in the moment where I should have been breaking through. When the bible says "He will be your strength in your time of weakness," I promise you it is not telling a lie.

Now, let's add all this up − fired, no savings, limited cash, fear, doubt and now uncertainty were all coming down on me. You want to know what God said at this pivotal place in my life? *FAST and PRAY for ninety days.* "Say what? God, how will You tell me to fast and pray when I'm about to lose everything including my mind!" Truth be told, I was resistant and contemplated brushing it off until I got a call from a friend saying, "Sis, I'm about to go on a ninety-day fast and I want you to do the fast with me."

"Uh??? Hello, you sure you meant to call me?" This was the thought going through my mind while holding the phone. "God, You're funny!" I finally agreed to the fast knowing that "some things only come by way of fasting and praying." I mean, what did I have to lose? Those ninety days, I began looking for locations, drawing out floor plans while consulting with God on what the name should be, the colors, and the type of atmosphere God wanted this salon to have. *God, where are the finances coming from?*

Two weeks passed and I ended up finding a location. Let's not forget we, and I mean the entire world, are in disarray due to the COVID-19 pandemic, but God opened a door for me and it's in the price point I prayed for! Not only that, but a couple weeks later unexpected finances were released and that gave me the chance to fill my emergency savings, my daughter's savings, my regular savings and checking, and the list goes on! All my bills were paid and paid forward. A faithful man abides in Blessings, and I'm a tither, so He held back the hand of the enemy for my namesake! I made sure to sow the seeds! Ok! Ok! Ok! Y'all get the point.

By the end of the ninety-day fasting and praying, the game had truly changed. The new salon was almost complete; it was fully furnished by God and those He sent my way to be a financial blessing. I was a week away from my Grand Opening of ESTEEM BEAUTY BAR! Never in a million years would I have imagined being the Boss in less than a year, eight months to be exact! I was so scared at one point, fearful that I didn't know enough, didn't think I was qualified, and I let others' opinions dictate whether I should jump or not, and they hadn't even jumped themselves.

Girl, I'm gonna be the sister, friend, auntie you need. I need you! Yes, you! To get up and get working so you can CHANGE THE GAME!! It's not just about you or for you, there are other lives connected to your DESTINY. If you don't start, they will never start. If you don't finish, they can never finish. God wants to use you to be the GAME CHANGER! You are their inspiration; people are watching you, GIRL! Whether it's good, bad, or ugly, they are watching for your response, your next move, and your next WIN! So that businesses plan you keep pushing to the side; that million dollar idea you were supposed to have patented; the clothing line you're supposed to create; get it back out and start working. Don't worry about finances; if God gave it to you, He will make the provision for it!

First things first though: Submit all your plans to the Lord and allow Him to lead and direct your path. Second thing: Kick fear, doubt, and other opinions out the door! Third thing: Fast and pray to gain clarity, focus, wisdom and knowledge, and the strength you're going to need to complete the assignment!

I'm rooting for you, **GAME CHANGER**!

If God be for YOU! Who can be against you!

About the Author:

Akya Canada is an author having self-published her first book titled *Single Moms Pray*. She is a trained hair stylist, professionally trained makeup artist and licensed cosmetologist. Also, she is an experienced public speaker, inspirational vocalist with a new single out called *I Can't Lose,* and actress who has toured the East coast and Canada.

Akya's dream is to inspire others to face their fears and make their dreams become reality. She knows that everything they need they already have.

Stay Connected with this Queen:

Follow her on this journey:

Flowpage.com/AkyaCanada

FB: @AkyaCanada

Instagram: @EsteemBB

FB: Esteem Beauty Bar

Youtube: Akya Canada

Download the HIT Single "*I Can't Lose*" on all music platforms

Go to Amazon and Order your copy today of my book *Single Mom's Pray*

NO MORE EXCUSES

MAGRIET POTGIETER

"He pulled away from them about a stone's throw, knelt down, and prayed, "Father, remove this cup from me. But please, not what I want. What do *you* want?" At once an angel from heaven was at his side, strengthening him. He prayed on all the harder. Sweat, wrung from him like drops of blood, poured off his face." **Luke 22:41-44 MSG**

The rumors you heard are true: Yes, we broke up, with no way of even thinking of ever reconciling again. It was a toxic, one-way relationship, with me giving everything up in this. I was voiceless, fearful, and totally paralyzed, emotionally and spiritually. Due to this, I was living my life the total opposite way of how God created us to live life.

A few of my excuses:

- I was adopted
- I'm a single mom
- I know abuse (emotional and verbal) all too well…

My list goes on.

Please note that this is still a part of my story. I'm not pretending that it's not a part of who I am. That it was not hard to get to this point. But I had to name it. I had to not only forgive, make peace, and move on, but also I had to embrace it. Every single excuse.

The definition of the word in the dictionary is as follows:

excuse

verb

/ɪkˈskjuːz,ɛkˈskjuːz/

1. Seek to lessen the blame attaching to (a fault or offence); try to justify.

2. Release (someone) from a duty or requirement.

For years, my excuses led me from one chapter to the other in dead ends. I really get why it took the Israelites 40 years to reach their

Promised Land; it took me 43 years... I spent 43 years being led in an emotional desert, being fed manna, experiencing the goodness of God, but making excuses not to enter the Promised Land God created me to enter and live in, not as a foreigner, but His daughter.

This was until one day… like the woman who was accused by the religion scholars and Pharisees of adultery and stoned, I was brought to a point through my sins and excuses. We read about Jesus' reaction to this in John 8:6-11 in the Message:

6-8 Jesus bent down and wrote with his finger in the dirt. They kept at him, badgering him. He straightened up and said, "The sinless one among you, go first: Throw the stone."

Bending down again, he wrote some more in the dirt.

9-10 Hearing that, they walked away, one after another, beginning with the oldest. The woman was left alone. Jesus stood up and spoke to her. "Woman, where are they? Does no one condemn you?"

11 "No one, Master."

"Neither do I," said Jesus. "Go on your way. From now on, don't sin."

Just like her, He did the same for me.

Excuses aren't something new to God. His first daughter He created, right after she sinned, instead of taking responsibility for her actions, made an excuse:

In Genesis 3: 13, we read: "GOD said to the Woman, 'What is this that you've done?'"

¹³ "The serpent seduced me," she said, "and I ate."

God knew she disobeyed Him, but still He asked her, "What is this that you've done?" For many years, He asked me, and I thought it was from a place of judgment, but it's not. It's from His Father's heart crying out, knowing how much my excuses kept me from the life of freedom and abundance He created me to live in. Like His initial plan for us in the Garden of Eden, Eve's excuses led to her not taking responsibility for her actions and led her away from the Garden and from the life of freedom she knew.

What are your excuses? What is God asking you today to admit? Not from a place of judgement, but from a Father's heart, crying out to His daughter, calling her back to His heart, His plan for her life. My excuses differ from yours. Let me show you a few excuses from daughters in God's Word that might resonate with yours (as it did with mine).

Excuse 1: It's impossible

Genesis 18 (The Message)

13-14 GOD said to Abraham, "Why did Sarah laugh saying, 'Me? Have a baby? An old woman like me?' Is anything too hard for GOD? I'll be back about this time next year and Sarah will have a baby."

15 Sarah lied. She said, "I didn't laugh," because she was afraid.

But he said, "Yes you did; you laughed."

Sarah laughed when she heard God's promise to her and Abraham. I'm not judging. She was 90 years old. I might have probably done the same. But once again, when God confronts her reaction, like Eve, Sarah doesn't admit and take responsibility in the situation. She chooses to lie and make an excuse. "I didn't laugh," she said, because she was afraid.

Our holy God did not punish her for laughing at Him. Instead, He said: "Yes you did; you laughed." Why would He do that? I think it was to emphasize that He knew she laughed at His promise, well knowing that He will fulfill it.

Are you laughing at a promise you are believing God to fulfill? Are you lying to God and yourself about it? God fulfilled His promise to Sarah and Abraham because He is good and faithful and just. If it wasn't impossible in the world's eyes and His children's, this wouldn't have been such an incredible miracle and answer to Sarah's prayers. Praise God in your impossible situation, dear daughter. What God has done for Sarah, He can and will do for you.

Excuse 2: I'd rather keep silent and not do anything about the situation

Esther 4 (The Message)

[12-14] When Hathach told Mordecai what Esther had said, Mordecai sent her this message: "Don't think that just because you live in the king's house, you're the one Jew who will get out of this alive. If you persist in staying silent at a time like this, help and deliverance will arrive for the Jews from someplace else; but you and your family will be wiped out. Who knows? Maybe you were made queen for just such a time as this."

Esther's life didn't start off easy by the loss of her parents. We read in Esther 2:7 in the Message: "Mordecai had reared his cousin Hadassah, otherwise known as Esther, since she had no father or mother. The girl had a good figure and a beautiful face. After her parents died, Mordecai had adopted her."

Being adopted myself, I know what a journey it was for me to truly feel I belonged somewhere. I'm not in any way suggesting that Mordecai, in any way, made Esther feel she didn't belong. But in my childhood years, I would wonder a lot how it would feel like to be raised by my biological parents. When I saw children with the same features as their parents, I would wonder how mine looked like.

Later on, in Esther's journey, she found herself in an extremely difficult position. Does she risk her life approaching her husband, the Persian king Ahasuerus (Xerxes I), to persuade him to retract an order for the general annihilation of Jews throughout the empire? Or keep silent, save herself and watch this in silence happening? Her uncle, the one who raised her, knew her possible excuse without her even saying it when he reached out to her about it in Esther 4 :12-14. What were you born to do? What are you silent about that will impact lives? Who knows, maybe you were made queen for just such a time as this.

Excuse 3: I made too many bad choices in my life

John 4 (The Message)

15 The woman said, "Sir, give me this water so I won't ever get thirsty, won't ever have to come back to this well again!"

16 He said, "Go call your husband and then come back."

17-18 "I have no husband," she said.

"That's nicely put: 'I have no husband.' You've had five husbands, and the man you're living with now isn't even your husband. You spoke the truth there, sure enough."

Like the woman at the well, I have made a lot of bad choices. She was shamed and ostracized by her community because of this. This is why she was drawing water in the middle of the day, under the scorching sun, to avoid anyone she knew and maybe any rude insults or dirty looks that came along with that. Maybe she wasn't taken aback that a Jew was speaking to her as Samaritan woman, but more of how respectful our Savior was talking to her. He knew her excuses. All five of them. And He helped her face it. One encounter with Jesus, and her life changed forever. She became the first evangelist for Jesus, sharing the good news of living water of amazing grace.

Are you standing at a well in your life? Jesus is standing there with you. Reaching out and asking you, just as he did to her: *Are you thirsty, and want the living water of grace?*

Excuse 4: I lost the one I loved the most

John 19: 24 -27 (The Message)

24-27 "While the soldiers were looking after themselves, Jesus' mother, his aunt, Mary the wife of Clopas, and Mary Magdalene stood at the foot of the cross. Jesus saw his mother and the disciple he loved standing near her. He said to his mother, 'Woman, here is your son.' Then to the disciple, 'Here is your mother.' From that moment, the disciple accepted her as his own mother."

I have a son. He is my heart. As a mother, I am crying as I write this. Crying for Maria, crying for every mother who has ever had to say goodbye to a child. I cannot imagine the pain she endured. I cannot even pretend. I do, however, know what it feels like to lose loved ones; I've had to say goodbye to both my parents: my mom died as a result of liver and kidney cancer and my dad passed away as a result of a heart attack a few years later. I remember sitting at his funeral, wanting to faint. The loss, the total grief, knowing I'm an orphan, left me totally devastated and heart broken.

My point with this chapter, and it's not an easy one to write, is that our greatest losses in life are the ones we were not prepared for. The ones we will never forget. The ones that make us want to cry at times when we have reminders of them. Those ones cannot be the reason we do not walk in our destiny. Jesus knew His mother. He knew how difficult it would be for her to process the loss of Him in her life. Even while He was dying, suffering on a cross for our sins, He was thinking of her... the woman who raised Him, who tended to His bruises when He fell as a little boy. The woman who now stood helpless in front of His cross as He was dying due to bruises caused by evil men.

Jesus knew she would need support to continue with her life after He was gone. If you are going through a difficult time after losing someone close to you, please reach out for support if you don't feel you are supported. Like His mother, Jesus doesn't want you to go through it alone. Our losses cannot prevent us from living our best lives. We honor God by praising Him through our tears. We honor Him by trusting that He knows best, even if we don't understand situations.

My prayer is that you, the reader, will realize how incredible you are in God's love story to the world. That He recognizes our excuses and still has so much grace for us. We were given free will. To choose. Either we let our excuses paralyze us and keep us in bondage, stuck to our past, stuck in hopeless situations, stuck in fear. Or we can turn our excuse into our reason.

We read in Luke 22: 41 – 44 in the Message where Jesus found Himself in front of the greatest excuse of His life:

41-44 "He pulled away from them about a stone's throw, knelt down, and prayed, 'Father, remove this cup from me. But please, not what I want. What do *you* want?' At once an angel from heaven was at his side, strengthening him. He prayed on all the harder. Sweat, wrung from him like drops of blood, poured off his face."

Jesus made a choice. Not from emotion, not from excuses, but His reason. His reason for coming to earth, His reason for dying on a cross, His reason for rising again and defeating the enemy, so that His daughters can live their lives in victory and bring glory to Him through their reason...Who set them free from lives hiding in the shadows of their excuses.

About the Author:

Magriet Potgieter is a passionate storyteller who believes in the power of embracing your life story. She now helps women do the same through her PR and Media Coaching business. She writes and speaks on various platforms. All for the glory of God.

Stay Connected with this Queen:

FB: https://www.facebook.com/magriet.potgieter.1/

IG: Write and Shine Through Your PR and Media Presence

HOLDING ON TO HOPE IN
TIMES OF CHANGE

MALA KENNEDY

***Hebrews 6:19 NLV: We have this hope as an anchor for the soul,
firm and secure. It enters the inner sanctuary behind the curtain.***

When COVID hit, I didn't know what to expect. At first, I didn't
believe it was as serious as people made out. A few weeks earlier, I
had booked to go to Bali on a retreat. This was my chance to focus
on some self-care and business strategy. An opportunity to get away
from the hectic life of being a mama & solopreneur. I didn't think

COVID would cancel my trip and yet God was giving me a lot of signs that it wasn't time.

Every time I tried to book my flights, the website would crash or time out. After several attempts, I knew this was a message for me. It was not my time to go overseas; I had work to do, and dreams to create. Soon after, COVID was upon us and we were in lockdown. Home with a 5-year-old and a 6-month-old baby fulltime, I found this challenging. It felt like my self-care was dissipating before my eyes. My half-hearted business felt like it was going to shrink even further. I say half-hearted because at the time I was still finding my feet in my business. I hadn't committed to showing up for myself. I was attracting clients who didn't want to invest with me. My Facebook group was an empty shell with no sense of community (or engagement). I could have given up; that would have felt natural to me at the time. Quitting and letting COVID win felt like the easy option. It was comfortable. However, I didn't quit. I rose, and I leaned into hope. I reflected on stories of other entrepreneurs who had risen in recessions. Hard times when everyone told them they couldn't, and I used them as my beacon of hope. If they could, why couldn't I?

I decided I could. The word "decision" means to kill off any other options. That was exactly what I was doing; I killed off the option to fail. My hope and determination was the only thing remaining. I knew I could, and I did.

Years earlier, after I had experienced postpartum depression when my son was born, when I was at my lowest, I had committed to healing. Hope was the one thing that kept me going. I had leaned into faith to pull myself out of depression. Experiencing vitiligo on my skin made me feel like I didn't belong. Watching my brown skin turn white made me feel like I wasn't good enough. It took a lot of hope, faith, and inner work to love and accept myself. My hope allowed me to open my heart, and decide to love myself, and in doing that I healed my life and became whole again. I learned to love my skin and see it as a gift from God.

Now, in 2020, I needed to surrender to the gifts of COVID. I discovered there were so many. The biggest one being time. Time has always felt like a precious commodity. Raising two kids can be all-consuming and I have been juggling being a mama with trying to run a business for years. My partner has also been working part-time whilst running his photography business. With very little support, it has felt like a game of tag trying to prioritize who gets to work on their business.

Before COVID, it was a scramble, early mornings, late nights (I am NOT a night person). We had scheduled days where we were both at home. We had allocated these as workdays, but something always seemed to get in the way. Whether it was swimming lessons, visitors, or lack of sleep. However, once we went into lockdown, there was enough time. We had more time to enjoy our presence together as a family. We also had plenty of time to focus on our businesses because as a team we could alternate who watched the kids.

I learned to prioritize my time using my tiny commitments method. Focusing on tiny, daily actions I could take to move the needle. This is something that created so many possibilities for me. By focusing on the next step with hope, trust, and surrender I would receive guidance on what to do next. I'd also build on my daily habits. I did this with incremental steps. 10 minutes of exercise on day 1, 11 minutes on day 2, and so on. This conditioned my mind and body to commit to my commitments. I'd follow through by creating tiny habits for success. I did it in a time when it could have been so easy to buy into the story that the world was falling apart.

My world wasn't falling apart because I believed it wasn't, and I believed it could. I invested in mentors, trusting in them, and trusting in me. I showed up online every day. I grew my Facebook group into a thriving hub, a (still growing) community of 700 plus members. I focused on my visibility. I had a vision of expanding my reach and I held on to hope that this could happen. Of course, it did with grace and ease. I was a guest on more than 10 podcasts during this time. It was a blessing to be able to share my story of self-acceptance and how it changed my life. I was even invited to be a guest speaker on two virtual summits. A dream-come-true that connected me with countless more soul-aligned women on the path to joy and freedom.

Before COVID, I had unresolved feelings of unworthiness. I felt like an imposter and whilst I had a handful of clients they weren't my dream clients. I was attracting scarcity clients who weren't soul-aligned. They were the clients who asked for discounts, who didn't show up on time (if at all), who never did the work and didn't see my value. It was as if they thought I was the reason for their lack of success. Their lack of self-responsibility and accountability became a reflection on me. They weren't open to receiving guidance or support. This became a direct reflection of my self-worth. I didn't value myself, so they didn't value me. I didn't have clear boundaries, so they had none. It was like looking in the mirror and it was painful.

As lockdown set in, I knew I wasn't available for this anymore. I knew there was more for me and I was ready and committed to making it happen. I had hope and I leaned in. I committed to working on my mindset because I felt like a fraud. I did a lot of tapping (emotional freedom technique) to clear my subconscious beliefs. Beliefs that I wasn't good enough. I tapped on them to reprogram them to beliefs that I was more than enough. I was ready to shift those limiting beliefs and write a new story for myself. A story where hope won and I was the creator of my dreams.

Every morning, I would work on my mindset because I felt like a fraud. I set aside time for my daily rituals. Meditating - my time to listen. Prayer - my time to ask, Tapping tapping - my time to clear and reprogram my subconscious. Journaling- my time to go even deeper and write out my vision. I would write the details of my success as the next-level Queen version of me. I'd journal on my dream client - who she was, her fears, hopes, and dreams, and how she showed up for herself. I tapped into her essence. This Queen became a reflection of me. This was a woman who was ready to invest in herself and committed to doing the work, and I knew she was on her way to me. I held on to this vision of her, with hope. I trusted in God, with a deep knowing that the Divine was taking care of everything, and He was.

Within weeks, I received a message from a dream client who was curious about working with me. After an amazing Discovery Call, she said a MASSIVE yes to working with me. My first VIP coaching client who was ready and excited. The whole process was easy and working with her was such a joy. I never had to wonder if she'd show up and I never doubted the value I added. This was divine guidance in a time where it felt like I should have failed. It felt like I should have people surrounding me who asked for discounts, but God gave me the opposite.

COVID was a time of opportunity for me; it blessed me with so many gifts. I was even able to hire an assistant to create more room for me to thrive in my zone of genius because I held on to my vision. I learned a valuable lesson during COVID. The circumstances of the world do not need to define your success. You define it, in partnership with God. During a pandemic, I tripled the size of my Facebook group. I became recognized as an authority in my coaching field. I attracted soul-aligned dream clients who were ready. I expanded my vision to the next level.

Hope was my key. I knew I could do anything with God's support, and I trusted in that. I leaned in. I gave myself space and time to do the inner work. Every day, I committed to sitting with God through meditation, prayer, and journaling. This strengthened my knowing. I committed to daily subconscious reprogramming. I used tapping to clear my subconscious beliefs that I was an imposter. I reframed my beliefs to know I was a successful Queen. I decided I was good enough and I chose God as my guide, and with that, I anchored my success in hope.

About the Author:

Mala helps female entrepreneurs show up and lead so they feel confident and successful. She loves supporting women to rewrite their worthiness story, permit themselves to be authentic, and create the life of their dreams. She is a mama, mindset coach, eft & reiki practitioner, writer, and meditation teacher in training. She is also trained in ontological coaching which integrates language, emotions, and body to integrate a new way of being.

Stay Connected with this Queen:

Social Media & Links: https://linktr.ee/malaloves

IG & FB @malaloves

THE DAY I LISTENED TO MY INNER SELF, I BIRTHED "SHE EXIST"

JENELLE HARRIS

The LORD is my shepherd, I lack nothing. He makes me lie down in green pastures, he leads me beside quiet waters, he refreshes my soul He guides me along the right paths for his name's sake. Even though I walk through the darkest valley,] I will fear no evil, for you are with me; your rod and your staff, they comfort me. You prepare a table before me in the presence of my enemies. You anoint my head with oil; my cup overflows. Surely your goodness and love will follow me all the days of my life, and I will dwell in the house of the LORD forever. **Psalm 23**

"SHE EXIST" has opened many avenues for me to help many women increase their self-esteem and become successful. In the process, I've become a professional marketing and management guru with vast experience in turning small businesses into multi-level Fortune 500 businesses. Over the last 15 years, my office has grown from a small part-time office to a multi-doctor practice. This growth is, in no small part, the results of dedication and tireless work.

Over this growth, I have demonstrated excellent organizational and interpersonal skills to develop office staff, as well as improve infrastructure within a business. Knowing that I once started small with my office, today, I'm glad that I've been able to take my small business office to over 5,000 per week. Now, this is something that every business should want to learn: how to increase their profits.

You see, I believe in progress! "If you can see it, believe it, then make it happen!" Being in the marketing and management field successfully for 15 years demonstrates the dedication and passion for this industry. Knowing what it takes when production is slow, makes me among the elite when it comes to success. I have helped a plethora of doctors, lawyers, and certified nurses over the years to find successful jobs in the medical industry.

Are you afraid to take risk?

Have you ever been in a position where you were afraid of making that move? You were in position, but fear was all over you? How many dreams came and left? How many times were you telling your friends and family "I am going to do this; I am going to do that?"

You are in a place of deep thoughts, you have a burning desire on the inside, but you cannot figure out what is wrong. You continue to research and study, but there is no action. Deep down, you are afraid of success not knowing you are afraid to step into your territory.

Being Courageous

Are you that individual who gets the job done, no matter what it takes? Are you that leader in your team who thinks outside the box? Are you that individual that takes notes? Do you put your words to action? Are you eager to learn new things? Are you hungry for knowledge?

Are we executing what we say?

To step in our territory, we must be courageous and willing to take risk. Our goal should be living out our full potential vs surviving. See, surviving tells me we are making sure the bills are paid and we have just enough to make ends meet. But when we decide to live out our true potential we become hungry for the things that we would not think we were hungry for. Often, we are waiting on God to save us with no action plan or we are waiting on destiny to surface.

Are we meeting new people? Are we reading new books? Are we getting involved with the people that are winning? Are we creating our own territory?

Are you asking yourself the right questions?

I like to ask questions to bring awareness to oneself for you to get uncomfortable. When I started asking myself questions such as **"Why" "Where" and "How,"** I began to answer the call to my own questions, and I chose to create my own success stories. I decided to step in my own territory with taking risk.

Growing in your territory

Have you ever found yourself in a place where you are expanding, and you realize your blueprint is finally coming together? The opportunities are knocking, but you are contemplating what keys you do have so you can unlock the right door. You're in a place where you are fed up with making wrong choices because it felt right, and the results were only lessons.

What are you willing to lose in order to gain?

Understanding your level of maturity and your level of growth can be challenging and a bit overwhelming. Especially when your career has a lot to do with interacting and working with people. You are learning how to navigate through someone else's opinions. Your success may never be understood, and you must position yourself in the right territory. Or you will have to make some hard decisions to walk your journey alone

The U-turn in your territory

Your journey can be a maze, and often your season may very well be 24 hours to a second and your decision are based on those circumstances. What is happening now VS what can happen. Your starting point was to be successful and that should be your only focus point

Developing key factors in your territory

What are your target factors? What is your game plan? What are some of your goals?

What do you need to get there? What is your definition of success? Who is on your team?

Surviving vs. Thriving

Surviving is a habit of being content and comfortable with our emotions along with our mindset. We often make excuses for our condition and that will justify why we are at that place in our territory.

Thriving makes you have desires, and having those desires will allow you to be uncomfortable for you to navigate through challenges. You will begin to reject traits of some surviving factors. You will begin to adapt effectively through the effects of life changes and fight through some uncertainty.

These are some thriving key factors:

Positive Perspective - Proactive Knowledge - Competence

About the Author:

Janelle is Founder and C.E.O of "SHE EXIST," a stellar mental health corporation which motivates women to take control of their life and business to the next level. She has built many based on her upbringing from her grandparents who demonstrated love and compassion for their community, neighbors, as well as church members.

Through the years, she has made an impact in her community by opening her home as a shelter to troubled women who either were less fortunate or just broken. While in her care, she uses her God-given talent to motivate and instill survival skills in many women while they are in the shelter and receiving care. She knows, she has a very huge heart for helping women and their family who are broken and in need of a cheerleader in their corner.

Her motivational talks have inspired women so much, that it led her to pursue and be a successful Life Coach and a Minister at Jones Miracle Temple. In her quest to continue my mission, she has followed her vision for" SHE EXIST" which was downloaded from God to help women in distress; to stay the course and keep God's plan (Jeremiah 29:11): "'For I know the plans I have for you,' declares the Lord, 'plans to prosper you and not to harm you, plans to give you a hope and a future.'"

This is a beautiful promise from God which gives us assurance for the future. Whatever may be your circumstances today, God's people can trust Him to change their tomorrow.

Stay Connected with this Queen:

For more information about me, please visit: www.sheexist.org

GOD'S DREAM WAS BIGGER

SHERRI CURRAN

"But seek first His kingdom and His righteousness, and all these things will be given to you as well." **Matthew 6:33 NIV**

I was raised in a loving home. We were in church at least twice a week and often had people in our home for Bible studies. I learned a lot about living a Christian life from the excellent example my parents were to me. In fact, my husband had a similar upbringing. You would expect that would set us up for an easy life, right?

My husband, Roger, and I enjoyed a snow-filled cabin get-away the week after our marriage. It was so beautiful in the mountains with all that glistening white. Sheer perfection until our vehicle was hit by a semi-truck. We were pulling off the road to put our SUV into 4-wheel drive when we were hit from behind. Don't worry; we weren't injured. But it was the beginning of our journey together, filled with challenges, difficulties, and disappointments.

I grew up in an entrepreneurial family. I like to say, "It runs through my veins." Though Roger wasn't raised that way, it ran thicker through his. He had already created multiple businesses before we had met in our mid-twenties. And just prior to our marriage, he had joined into partnership on a business in the San Francisco Bay Area. It had been a huge opportunity for him and his parents supported it, and him, by leveraging their home.

After salvaging the remainder of our honeymoon, we returned to our new home in our bent-up SUV. We were prepared to put it behind us and pioneer onward toward our new adventure together. That first day back to work, Roger's partner informed him that the business was not doing well enough to support two owners and that one would have to buy the other out, in order to continue.

Because of my in-laws' home being leveraged, my husband drew the short end of the stick. The next thing I knew, we were getting another loan to buy out the partner. This was a huge step for a young newly married couple. This would be our next obstacle to push through in our journey together.

I had been trained in bookkeeping, so we decided I should quit my job to help support our new struggling business. We were determined to give this everything we had in order for it to be successful! On the other hand though, we were putting all our eggs in one basket.

I'm sure we sought the Lord and prayed during that time. But I think we also made a lot of knee-jerk reactions, seemingly to be our only options. We both desired to do His will, but knew we needed to work as hard as we possibly could during that time.

Because of the hard work and long hours we were putting in, our next challenge was a shock to us. It was especially surprising because we didn't know you could get pregnant while taking birth control pills. But here we were staring at the test results. We were going to be adding another member to our newly formed family.

We were adjusting to our new "normal" and planning our future for our family and business. It was October 17, 1989. If you lived in Northern California around the time or were settling in to watch the *World Series* that day, you know exactly what I'm going to tell you. That was the day of the Loma Prieta earthquake that struck the San Francisco Bay Area.

I rose from my couch, 3-month pregnant. Our stereo speakers had fallen off the entertainment center as the shower doors crashed from side to side. I was terrified! Thankfully that day, Roger was close to home and arrived there soon after it happened. He typically made deliveries all over the Bay Area and would cross the bay multiple times a week using the Bay Bridge. On this day, a section of that bridge had collapsed. How thankful we were to have been spared that devastation. We three were healthy and whole.

Our business had also been spared any major damage, or so we thought. The damage was to come. Day after day, week after week, we struggled to get back to business as usual. Unfortunately, the area was shut down for months. No one was buying what we were selling. Our already struggling business could not take much more!

Our business continued to struggle, trying to survive the challenges it had encountered. During this time, our first son, David, was born. He was, and still is, a joy to our hearts. We wouldn't have planned to have him during this season, but God had blessed us with a better plan.

A year passed after the earthquake. We knew we were going to have to make another tough decision. Our next challenge would be a move. Three months later, we were getting settled in our new place in Central Valley, California. Rent for our business was going to be so much less there, though the travel would be hours more a day. It was a trade-off we decided we had to make. But we didn't realize the toll it would take on business connections and on our marriage. We seemed to be losing ground on all sides.

In an effort to plant roots and get settled there, we bought a home. Roger had been doing some renovations, closing in a porch to use as a workshop. It was a Sunday afternoon in late September and he was laying down the last section of carpet in the newly formed room. David and I were anxious for him to be done, so we joined him and watched as he was finishing up.

Suddenly, I heard a hiss and a gasp. Something inside of me sensed the danger, so I immediately rose to my feet and snatched up my son, just as the flames reached us. The pilot light from the water heater in the next room had ignited the glue fumes from the carpet installation. In an instant, Roger was running out one door, David and I another.

What felt like a close-call, ended up being much worse than we thought.

I'll spare you the details of life in the burn center. It wasn't a pleasant journey, but we are eternally grateful for the care we received. Miraculously, Roger survived after having burned 40% of his body and a detection that his lungs had been burned. What was expected to have been a 6-month treatment and recovery, ended with him walking out of the hospital in 30 days. David and I, having been released after 7 days, were both anxious to see him and nervous to discover how we could take care of each other in the days to come. We learned to manage that, but getting the business back to normal was the bigger challenge.

It didn't take long, only a few months, to realize that our business was not going to survive. My in-laws had to make a sacrificial decision to sell their house and relocate, in order to cover our debt. They exemplified to us an earthly glimpse of what Christ did by making that ultimate sacrifice to pay for our sins. We are eternally grateful for our parents and to our Lord.

We needed a fresh start. We hoped this would also help our marriage to survive. But the damage seemed too great. We had just moved to another state and started attending a church. Roger was out drumming up some work when he ran into a guy who had led a class we had attended the Sunday before. With a heavy heart for our relationship, he asked this man if he knew a good marriage counselor. As the Lord ordained, this man and his wife were marriage ministry leaders in the area. This set our marriage off in the right direction and placed us on a path of much-needed spiritual growth.

The next several years were rebuilding years. We started many more businesses and entered into other partnerships, which came with ups and downs. With an improved relationship, we decided to have our second son, Matthew. Another huge blessing from the Lord. We reflected over our previous 5 years and saw God's hand miraculously providing us our first child to help keep us together, until we could get back on track.

We continued in entrepreneurship and making moves to advance, but parenthood was our new passion. We felt God calling us to homeschool and to have more children. Seven years after Matthew was born, we had another son, Daniel, and a year and a half later, Jonathan. Four boys! What an adventure! Those years of running businesses, homeschooling, and raising kids were hard, but years that I will treasure for the rest of my life.

Roger eventually got into construction and real estate investing. This profession contributed to several of our moves, but usually just within the same general area. Until the economic crash of 2008. At the beginning of that year, Roger had 8 houses in addition to some other projects he had lined up to build. By September, we had lost all of our projects as well as every credit line we had established for doing business. We knew we were going to have to make another drastic change.

We had learned our lesson and earnestly sought the Lord for this particular move. Hurricane Ike had hit the Houston area on September 13, 2008, so we made a scouting trip in October to determine if this would be a good move for our precious family. Our boys had never lived in such a large city and we were moving halfway across the country. We were convinced this was the direction God had for us and were officially in Texas by February.

This move instigated a huge desire in me to grow spiritually. So I sought out godly women at my new church and developed a love for ministry and missions. After 25 years of homeschooling, I looked forward to spending my empty-nest stage of life devoting all my time to pouring into other people's lives one-by-one through Bible Study, missions, and other volunteer work. This was my dream, now that my boys had grown into wonderful godly men and no longer needed me like they did before.

My dream died, though, the day my husband and I sat down for a conversation about our future. Our business deals and financial sacrifices we had over the years had not given us the nest egg we needed for our empty-nest. We had worked for 30 years, just to have to work for the rest. Don't get me wrong; having focused on our boys had been the right decision, but now what were we going to do about income and retirement?

I spent a few weeks crying, praying and seeking the Lord for direction. I hoped that He would have a plan that could be just as purposeful and rewarding as MY plan was. He assured me that He did! Jeremiah 29:11. He wanted me to impact many more lives than I could have imagined.

His plan was for me to utilize my training and 30 years' experience in bookkeeping to start a business. This was not going to be just a side hustle, but a way to support multiple owners to success in their businesses. He urged me to keep Him first and seek Him for direction every step of the way. "But seek first His kingdom and His righteousness, and all these things will be given to you as well." Matthew 6:33. And when discouragement or fear would creep in, to look to Him, like Peter did as he stepped out of the boat and walked on the water with Jesus.

Looking back over the difficult years, I recognize that what the enemy meant for evil, God was going to use for good. He had allowed those years of challenges to refine me and prepare me for this. God's dream for me was BIGGER!

About the Author:

Sheri is a Professional Bookkeeper who works with small business owners to significantly reduce their stress and time spent on managing their financial data. From her 30+ years of experience managing bookkeeping for small businesses, Sheri understands the challenges of the busy entrepreneur. When "wearing all the hats" becomes impossible, she steps in to relieve that burden of managing the financial data of their growing business.

Stay Connected with this Queen:

CurranBookkeeping.com

LEAVING SIX FIGURES IN FAITH

TRACY TATE JONES

I can do all things through Christ who strengthens me.
Philippians 4:13.

Hello, Hello, Hello, Queens. I am Tracy L. Tate Jones, CEO of TLJ
Professional Services, where we are About All Things Financial ™.
We provide services in bookkeeping, accounting, taxes for business
and individuals, life and health insurance for business and
individuals, business coaching, business formation and business
funding for well-established businesses. I am here to share with you

my journey of leaving a six-figure corporate job to growing my six-figure business within one year. www.tljprofessionalservices.com

First things first. I worked for a Real Estate Investment Trust (REIT) in San Francisco, CA for eleven and a half years, starting in their second year of business. There were approximately three hundred employees then and my department had only two of us. The company had grown to over fifteen hundred employees by the time I left. There had been five or six acquisitions and I was the Director of Accounts Payable in the Accounting Department. I created departmental policies, procedures, system implementations and eventually grew the department to twelve employees under me.

Throughout the course of these eleven years, not once, not twice, but three times, I applied for promotions that were delayed. It was given, but not until maybe the year after it was supposed to be given. I was even tasked to write my own promotions. There was a lady that had been there a couple of years before me that didn't have a department or a team to oversee, but because she was there before me, our manager seemed to think if he promoted me, he had to promote her too. Well, there were times that I qualified, but she did not, so I strongly believe that caused two of the delayed promotions. I caught on to it by promotion number two, but initially thought maybe I had not done something right in the write-up. Maybe there was really no need to promote. That was the promotion from Supervisor to Manager.

By the time I got promoted from Manager to Senior Manager, it was very clear to me that he kept us on the same platform. I called a meeting with my manager to flat-out ask him, "Are you keeping me and this employee on the same promotion schedule? We are not on the same playing field. I run the Accounts Payable Department; she prepares financial statements and one staff." By then, I had grown the department to six staff. He flat-out denied it and said he would never do that.

It was in our last acquisition and restructuring of the company when they let go of some property managers, so my team had to pick up some of the slack. We automated and implemented new processes and systems. Everyone on the team that implemented the system got a promotion that year but me. I didn't understand it, but was told that promotions were not being made in the Accounting Department; however, our International counterparts did get promotions, including the ones that were on the project that I implemented, so why wouldn't I be the one to get recognition? I was the one in charge of it. It was then that I called that meeting to say something was not right. I became bitter and I knew it was time for me to go.

During that time, I also worked my bookkeeping and tax business, but had converted from a Sole Proprietor to a Corporation in 2014 to include business formation and coaching, as well as life insurance. By 2017, I had a bad a taste in my mouth about everything that had happened with my promotions but did not have the confidence to walk away. I am also the type of person that takes my job and career seriously, so I wasn't going to leave the position after implementing the new system.

I finally got the promotion after I called a meeting with the Controller. I found out then that my promotion request was never submitted for consideration. I was livid. Although he threw my manager under the bus with the statement, he was not cleared either. As the head of the department, if he saw there were promotions that should have been submitted that had not been, why wouldn't he say something? Besides that, it was a title change without the financial backing to it. It was then that I was determined to find out how I was going to exit, but did not have a clue. I also knew I did not want to work for anyone. I even went on a job interview and sabotaged it because I knew in my spirit, in my heart, I did not want to work for anyone anymore because of the corporate glass ceiling, because of the games they play and the politics. No one would ever be able to dictate my advancement or success, my time off or my worth.

In July 2017, I was in a rear end car accident, but I went back to work a week later. By January 2018, I could not feel my right side anymore and I could not use my arm at all. I knew then that the Lord had sat me down but did not know the purpose. During my disability, there were many days I stayed in bed, was in agonizing pain and was heavily medicated. I barely worked my bookkeeping business and outsourced a lot of the work. I went from a thirty-thousand-dollar business to a ninety-thousand-dollar business in the year, I was on disability. I was completely surprised to see the growth and with me partially working the business. I immediately thought about how much my business could grow if I dedicated the time and efforts I put into the REIT, into my own business.

After being off work for a year on disability, in February 2019 I returned to a department that was different and my team's enthusiasm and dedication was different, as they had become disgruntled with leadership. The time I put into building my department, the people in my department and building them up for the past 10 years, everything changed. I was not OK with it and it just seemed like there was no compliance and regulations were compromised. As I stated before, I take pride in my work and career so am a stickler to rules and I hold everybody accountable. They had made decisions that were way off base, did not follow compliance, and did not follow the procedures that were in place, so I was not going to be accountable for the mess they made.

Another deciding factor was, upon my return my annual stock award and bonus had been withheld, although it was always part of the salary package in prior years. How can you say an employment package or salary package includes this, this and this, but withhold it when I return to work, doing the same position, doing the same work? I no longer had stock and only ten percent of my annual bonus, although I was helping while I was out answering calls and questions. Within six months of returning, I gave my two-week notice. I set out on my entrepreneur journey and I stepped out on Faith with thirty thousand dollars in my 401k retirement plan and nothing saved. I could not pretend to be okay in my position any longer, so I left.

In my transition, still nervous because I had always worked for someone else, I had been an employee of a second company, a private company that I worked with before I went to the corporate position. When I still worked at the REIT, I worked with them as a supplement to my income. I converted from being an employee with them to them being a client of mine. That helped boost my income and was an easy conversion. I was also able to convert the REIT to a client as well. Regardless of me being out for a year prior, I had the historical knowledge of the company's past eleven years. Even now, a year later, they still call me for my knowledge and expertise.

In July 2019, I had attended a conference in Atlanta called Traffic Sales and Profit with Lamar Tyler and joined the Facebook group. When I tell you black excellence in that group alone changed my whole mindset, believe me. My mindset about what I can do and what my capabilities are in business. There are black-owned businesses from startups all the way to multi-millionaires. It gave me the encouragement to know that I could do it.

I have always been a behind-the-scenes type of person and never in the limelight, but they gave me the tools to use. I don't use the concept; if they can do it, I can do it. I had stepped out on Faith and knew God was making a way for me to pursue my true calling of helping others. I have been able to dedicate some time to my nonprofit, Beat the Street, Inc, a resource center for young adults in California for youth ages thirteen to twenty-nine around education, employment and life skills. I started on that journey by Faith in 2005 and I have been carrying it ever since.

I am pleased, happy, and ecstatic to say within twelve months of leaving my six-figure corporate job, not only have I surpassed the salary, exceeded the annual bonus, and stock award, but have also exceeded the supplemental income from my bookkeeping business. So, when I tell you I stepped out on faith and walked away from that corporate job with only thirty thousand in my 401k, I have not missed a beat. God has been and continues to make way for me. I am being connected to other people that have networks in need of my services and can use my expertise. I bring over thirty-five years of experience in accounting, bookkeeping, and taxes. I have a Master's degree in Business, in Accounting, as well as a Master's degree in Public Administration.

I have been blessed and honored to talk about my experiences and about finances on various platforms, about the glory of God and what he could do for you. I could not help but say yes to Mrs. Nakita, Queen. I'm releasing my first course, *Optimizing Your Tax Deductions for Entrepreneurs and Small Businesses* in November 2020 to help them in their journey of discovering their mission, vision, and purpose in business from a financial standpoint, from a mindset standpoint, as well as from a business standpoint. I hope you enjoyed my story of leaving six-figures in faith

About the Author:

Stay Connected with this Queen on Social Media:

Follow us on Facebook, Instagram and LinkedIn: TLJ Professional Services Inc

THE POWER OF RISING IN RESILIENCE: FINDING INNER PEACE THROUGH GRATITUDE AND MINDFULNESS

STEPHANIE MOORE

Acts 16: 31 (NIV) - "They replied, 'Believe in the Lord Jesus, and you will be saved - you and your household.'"

The anticipation and excitement around graduating college are one of those unmatched feelings that I could not fully describe. As May 4th, 2019 got closer and closer, though I was ready to close this 5-year long chapter that had molded so much of my mind, being, and experience as an emerging young adult, my mind felt like it was on autopilot due to the endless tasks I had to take care of to walk across the stage gracefully.

I don't think it fully registered that I had graduated with my Bachelor of Social Work from the University of Alabama until that Monday morning when all of the "hype" died down. It was indeed at that moment I took the most resounding sigh of relief. In this robust exhale, I could feel every late night or early morning I spent working on assignments, the battles with anxiety, depression, and imposter syndrome, the stress from the weight of my world on my shoulders, every tear I had shed, the hustle and ambition I had birthed into Freelancer Magazine, an online publication I started and ran from 2016-2018 during my time in undergrad, and every social media internship I took on to build my resume and experience because I knew that, outside of my degree in social work, I had a deep passion and purpose for the marketing industry. To have that level of lighthearted energy encapsulated in my spirit when all it had known was tension, worry, anxiety, and stress was refreshing, but, mentally, I didn't expect it to be so short-lived. I didn't expect imposter syndrome to invite itself back into my life when I thought we had said farewell and mutually agreed to part ways because like an unhealthy attachment or relationship, this negative thought cycle made me lose sight of who I was.

See, I don't think there is enough conversation around a student's identity and how it has carried people, including myself, throughout our lives. From pre-school through college graduation, our identity can be strongly connected to our status as a student. We find ourselves bound by the success of our assignments, roles, and participation in clubs, honor societies, and student organizations, and many other accolades that we can attribute to our academic career throughout our lives, but what happens when being a student stops? That is where my mind wandered and along with imposter syndrome came post-graduate depression. I was no longer in a state of working, consistently being productive, or producing assignments for courses. I was in a state of just being, and it was a shock to my system that left me feeling uncomfortable.

After graduation is when you're supposed to start applying for jobs within your respective industry, hitting the ground early, and trying to get your feet wet. There is supposed to be a level of joy, a spark, a jolt, as you envision yourself working within your field. I didn't feel that. I was met with an internal conversation of, "What do I do now?" "What is my purpose?" and "I don't even know where to begin." Since February 2019, I worked at a call center in Tuscaloosa, Alabama. I would be until June 2019, but the long hours and restrictive shift guidelines became mentally exhausting and caused me to feel like a prisoner in my job, mind, and body.

Following graduation, I decided to take a week off for rest before resuming back to work on May 13th. Still, the more I continued to work at the call center, the more my body just energetically was not aligning with the work culture or my coworkers. I can't recall the exact day, but I will never forget the feeling. I woke up one morning for an 8:00 AM - 4:30 PM shift, and I found myself crying in the bathroom before I could even prepare myself for work. I felt so defeated and depleted.

I kept applying for job after job in the social work industry and the social media industry, but yielded no results. I had even been working with a staffing agency in Birmingham, Alabama. Still, because I didn't have a relevant degree in marketing or social media, many companies were saying "no" despite my long experience. My representative once told me that a company did not like that I had noted myself as "CEO of Freelancer Magazine" on my resume, even though it was MY magazine that I had built from the ground up! That was the reason they decided to forgo my application. All of the frustration from setback after setback had compounded in my mind and my heart. The wall of suppression that I had built was cracking; the release of my tears was slipping through the foundation, and by my lunch break? The wall had crumbled.

I was on a three-way call with my mom and dad, chest heavy, tears streaming endlessly down my face, and a lump in my throat that felt like a wail or a powerful scream could only release it, but because I was in a work environment, I had to contain myself. I expressed my frustration, anger, impatience, and constant questioning of "why me?" to my parents. Ultimately, I wanted to admit myself to DCH North Habor, a mental health facility, again. For context, I say, "again," because I was admitted to North Habor in November 2017 after having a mental breakdown at 3:00 AM during my tenure in undergrad.

Depression and anxiety had been, and still is, a recurring battle of mine. Since 2016, up until June 2019, I tried to find the right medication for my depression and anxiety, but nothing seemed to work for me. I even journeyed into GeneSight testing, which allows you to see which medications, based on your mental health diagnosis, align with your body chemistry. I thought I had FINALLY made a breakthrough in September and October 2017, but after being prescribed 50 mg of Seroquel, that reality changed quickly.

On the early morning of November 15th, 2017, I found myself in the middle of my floor, numb, unemotional, and withdrawn. At the time, my boyfriend had woken up to find me on the floor, concerned as to what was going on. I couldn't even verbalize what I was feeling or what I was thinking because it felt like emptiness. Nothingness. I just burst into tears, profusely picking at the edges of my hair because I felt like I was losing my mind. I ended up calling my parents to let them know that my boyfriend was going to drive me to DCH North Harbor and I would be admitting myself because I couldn't see myself sleeping this off.

As scary as the experience was for me, to have my boyfriend by my side, offering me comfort and support until my family could arrive, I felt at peace. I'll never forget, as I was waiting to be properly admitted, he asked me if I could live anywhere in the world right now, where it would be. Because I had been thinking about relocating to Texas after graduation, that's what I told him. This spiraled into a conversation about his time during childhood when he lived in Texas. The conversation was light, funny, and nostalgic. I was able to calm my anxious mind and breathe.

When my parents had finally arrived, I embraced them so tightly. Every single one of my five senses was elated to see them. Seeing my family, hearing their sweet voices, feeling their warmth, smelling the familiar scents of my loved ones, touching and holding their hands, and tasting nostalgia, safety, and freedom, my soul had a level of inner peace that no mental health facility could bring me. I remained under the care of North Harbor for 24 hours and started treatment under new medication, as well as a new therapist.

Ultimately, instead of admitting myself to North Harbor again, I decided to allow myself to embrace my feelings in the moment and eventually, I was applying for jobs again. This time, however, I applied for jobs with the mindset of *what is meant for me will flow to me effortlessly and what is delayed, does not necessarily mean it is denied.* Before long, I applied for a Drug Prevention Specialist position with a local non-profit organization and I began working for them in June 2019. Being able to leave to call center and start my first full-time position in the field of social work was just the jumpstart I needed to help start the next chapter of my life, post-graduate.

By August 2019, I had moved out of student living and into a two-bedroom apartment with my younger sister, who was attending The University of Alabama on a pre-law track. With a new job and a new living environment, everything just felt aligned. With eagerness in my heart, I was ready to venture into the field of drug prevention, something that I was not well-versed in, but was willing to be adaptable. I was enjoying my work family, the work and support I was extending to Tuscaloosa County, as well as other surrounding counties. I finally felt like life was moving in the right decision, but honey, sometimes I felt like God was out to get me and I could NEVER be happy beyond a moment.

What started out as a positive work environment slowly boiled into an environment that was brewing with micro aggressions, nepotism, micromanagement, and disorganization. The stress and toxicity of this job became physical. I would wake up with jaw pain and dull headaches due to grinding my teeth from stress and anxiety and sometimes found myself having crying spells while getting ready to work. The amount of mental and physical wear on my body was not worth $13/hr with no benefits (thankfully, I was still covered by my parents). Energetically, my spirit needed to purge, once again, from something I thought was destined for me, but would be a lesson learned and a stepping stone.

Physically and mentally withdrawn from my current positon, I decided to be proactive again in praying and applying for more positions within the social work field. I vividly remember praying to God, telling Him that whatever He had planned next for me, I was willing to adjust and adapt. After applying to several positions, I heard back from a company that was looking for a Case Manager for an emerging program they were looking to start within their agency. The interview was PHENOMENAL! My interview was slotted at 2:30 PM and I didn't leave the office until 5:00 PM. With an interview lasting 2.5 hours? I was confident the job was already mine and I was speaking it into existence every single day until I got the call with a job offer.

In mid-September 2019, a couple of weeks after I had interviewed with the new company, I was sitting at the desk of my then current position when I received the phone call I had been WAITING for. I received the job offer, a pay increase, and a benefits package. I couldn't do anything but cry and thank God for rescuing me from my current job environment and blessing me with something better.

Cheerful and confident in this new direction God was placing me in, I typed up my two weeks' notice, and by October 3rd, 2019, I would be saying goodbye to my job as a Drug Prevention Specialist and ushered in the new Case Manager position I had fallen in love with already. You remember how I said I felt that I could never be happy beyond a moment? Well, here we are again. As I was heading out the door for work during my last week, I got a phone call from the company saying that my job offer had been rescinded and they decided to move forward with another candidate. I don't think my mind or body was prepared for that level of attack, because that's what it felt like. I was reeling with anxiety. I could barely breathe, let alone see through my own tears, driving, as I tried to release as much as I could before walking into work to save face.

I pulled into the parking lot, called my parents, and I couldn't help but to break down. The frustration, anger, and overwhelming emotions took over my entire being. I was numb; I didn't care anymore because it felt like no matter how hard I tried, nothing was working in my favor. I honestly felt like I wasn't good enough. Though the news was hard on me and my parents, I found solace in their words as they reassured me that everything was going to be okay, regardless of if I couldn't see it in that moment. It felt like college all over again: being financially dependent on my parents, not having a job, trying to find yet another direction in my life.

Outside of losing the job offer and not having a proper full-time position to fall back on, I was hopeful that one of the social media marketing contract positions I had held since December 2018 would turn into a full-time role. However, I was informed by my supervisor, who ran her own counseling centers in which I was doing the social media for, that my position would be ending by December 2019. Due to the level of dysfunction I was experiencing at my full-time job, I wasn't able to properly commit the time and resources I desired to her businesses. We were both well aware of this, but I was hoping that with me having more free time, I could dedicate more energy into her social media marketing. Eventually, we had a conversation where we mutually decided that it would be wise to end my contract because the reality of it was, I could be offered a new job the next day, the next week, or the next month, but with that level of uncertainty, her business and her finances could not take that risk if I would not be able to fully commit to the demands of the position. Once again, I had experienced a loss.

I felt triggered just about every single day. What was even more triggering was by October 5th, 2019, I was in that state of just being that I had felt post-graduation. I didn't know how to sit still because all my mind and body had ever known was work or school. Most days, I felt emotionally heavy, worthless, sad, and just empty. I started to feel that I had no purpose or direction in my life. I was simply just here, existing, but not living or thriving.

In a state of trying to build a sense of normalcy to my life, I decided to take a nice, hot shower while listening to Sarah Jakes Roberts' sermon, "A Tight Spot." Before selecting this sermon to watch, I prayed and asked God to lead me to a word that was meant for me. Energetically, I felt drawn to this particular sermon and I listened to it while I showered. I didn't expect to have church in the shower, but my God it felt good. It felt good to praise and worship, cry, release, pray, and just have personal time with God, even with it being in the shower. Sarah was speaking from the book of Acts and one of the scriptures she read was **Acts 16: 31 (NIV) - "They replied, 'Believe in the Lord Jesus, and you will be saved - you and your household.'"** They referred to Paul and Silas. Just like Paul and Silas, who experienced pain, imprisonment, strife, and were in a tight spot of their own, I, too, was in a season of a tight spot.

As I continued to listen and meditate on Sarah's sermon, I began speaking to myself. Telling myself that *I won't waste my time in self-pity, doubt, blame, or questioning God and His method. I will continue to praise Him in advance and thank Him over and over again. I told myself that I invite God into this tight spot with me so that He may stretch me and mold me into the woman I am destined to become. This tight spot isn't meant for me to stay complacent or to get claustrophobic, but it's meant for God to stretch this tight spot and make room for the blessings to come. My purpose is greater than this moment; I am greater than this moment. I am not less than; I am not an imposter. I know who I am and God knows who I am. He knows my heart and my vision. The method is the only thing that has changed, but the vision is still the same. I'm willing to adjust and adhere to the change in His method. This is a season of transformation and healing, yes, but it is also a season of discomfort. In order to elevate, God is going to make things uncomfortable and stretch me to help me grow. I won't give up, I won't quit, and I won't go back to the ways of my past in defeat and sorrow. I will keep my head held high and continue to smile through this process and remain patient and faithful through it all.*

Having this inner dialogue with myself and God was ministry to my soul.

On my productive days, I applied for jobs, while also thinking more about my future and what that would look like for me. Did I want to attend graduate school for social work or for marketing? Did I want to leave the world of social work behind and embark into the social media marketing industry heavily? How do I want to utilize my social work degree? During these months, I had preliminary thoughts about starting my own social media marketing services, as well as using my social work degree to venture into life coaching, but I had never sat down with the thoughts and looked deeper. On the days when I felt I just wanted to rest, I did just that and nothing else. All guilt-free! If I found myself slipping into a state of sadness or emotional heaviness, I allowed myself to acknowledge those feelings, navigate through them, and heal them versus suppressing them or allowing them to fester. I had to remind myself that even when I do have good days, there will always be bad days, but it's about HOW you manage those bad days. That is what matters.

During my time being unemployed, I began showing myself more grace and compassion with my still moments. I didn't view myself as lazy, unproductive, or misguided. I told myself that this time was needed for me because for the past 5 years of my life, I didn't know how to just be with myself. I was always working or keeping myself busy. I was taking 15 credit hours each semester; for two years, I was running an online publication. For a period of time, I was juggling my magazine, school, and 2 part-time jobs, and some semesters I was juggling 15 credit hours and social media internships. The only time I truly rested was during the holidays when I was with family or when I laid my head down on my pillow to sleep. My body needed to know rest. My spirit needed to know rest because I was not honoring myself enough, nor truly listening to the needs and demands of my body while I was so quick to fulfill the demands and needs of other people.

It was also during my season of transformation and discomfort that I realized that the conversation around grieving the loss of a job was taboo. I think what most people don't realize is that job loss is most definitely a form of grief. You have to allow yourself to grieve the loss of the job, accept the feelings that came with the job loss, but don't allow your emotions to take the driver's seat. Living in uncertainty is scary and tough, but having faith is 100% KEY! Though the next move is uncertain, choosing to keep your faith strong and optimism high is optimal because this period of life is a temporary setback for major blessings and manifestations to come into your life. The time you have while being unemployed can be used to be proactive about your future, but also a time to really re-ground yourself, tap into yourself more, create routines, nurture passions and talents that may have been stifled while in the workplace, and really just become ONE with yourself again because sometimes we lose ourselves within our positions. Creating a thriving mental environment for yourself with the free time you will have will be a great foundation for the next chapter of your life. **Remember, you're not less than, worthless, and your value does not decrease because of unemployment. Be kind to yourself, nurture, and love yourself during this process! You will find a position that will not only cater to your values and expectations as an employee, but will also align with the mission of the company.**

By the end of October, a few weeks into my unemployment, I had been contacted by an old friend just to check in and see how I was doing. I gave him the entire rundown on how life had been post-graduation and he empathized with me and my current situation. He also informed me that his company, a social media agency in Birmingham, was currently hiring for an Account Manager and that I should forward him, and his bosses, my most recent resume and cover letter for consideration on the position. Now, I had always had the goal of working within an agency for social media versus doing strictly freelancer or contract work, because I told myself that I would love to know what working within an agency is like for social media, as well as what I could learn.

I polished my resume, cover letter, and even built a portfolio on Wix to help build my case for this position. By November 2019, I was called in for an interview, which I SLAYED, and in December 2019, I received one of the best Christmas gifts I could ask for: a job offer with DOUBLE the salary I was making at my previous employer, health benefits, a 401(k) plan, bonuses, learning credit, and a plethora of other benefits that left me in a state of euphoria and ready to start off 2020 STRONG!

On January 13th, 2020, I was employed again as an Account Manager for a reputable social media agency in Birmingham, Alabama. Having that hard shift of going into the office every day to working from home since March 2020 due to COVID-19, was definitely a mental shock. Trying to find a work-life balance when all of your life and work is now at home was a challenge. My productivity and energy suffered at times, but I was working diligently to try and build a system that would set me up for success as an Account Manager, as well as my clients. What was also a blessing was the endless access to resources that were becoming available due to the pandemic. From certifications to courses to webinars to free resources and guides, I felt the bittersweet energy of this pandemic.

While working under this agency, I can honestly say that as I navigated through the company and the position, I had built an arsenal of knowledge on the industry that I don't believe I would have learned on my own. I felt inspired by my co-workers who, outside of working for the agency full-time, had their own side hustles in the creative industry. Seeing them thrive in their element gave me the push I needed to think intensely about my business.

In March, I started thinking of various business names, and in May/June, I was brainstorming different content ideas I would have for my social media marketing and life coaching businesses, as well as the different services I would offer. In June, I told myself, "Okay, we'll take the month of July to prep and plan and then execute and launch social media services in August. For life coaching, we'll start the certification courses in August and launch those services by January 2021." June turned into July, July turned into August, and before I knew it, I was all talk and no action.

Fear has a crazy way of holding you back from taking a leap of faith and channeling into full-time entrepreneurship. It's August and I knew where I was standing in my life currently: a full-time job working from home that was slowly but surely misaligning with my mindset, spirit, and energy, two social media marketing contract positions that were paying very well and I absolutely loved, and the names of my businesses, as well as the direction for each, already mapped out. I had decided on Moore Creative Media for my social media marketing services and Moore 2 Life Coaching & Wellness for my life coaching services. So, knowing all of this, what was I fearful of?

I had been going back and forth with quitting my full-time job and embracing full-time entrepreneurship while still working under my contract positions. I believe the root of my fear was fearing being in the same place I was in around the same time in 2019: unemployed and misguided. I wasn't going to allow my mind to travel back in time when the present moment, as well as my future, was the only thing that mattered.

One night, I softly played Yolanda Adams' *Open My Hear"* and I spoke with God. I told Him that I wanted to advance my faith and start practicing the art of radical faith. Believing that regardless of what the circumstances may look like in that moment, that greater is coming for me and I cannot question it, nor shake my faith. After having this intentional conversation with God, the blessings came FLOODING in! By the end of August, I had landed a business coach and a mindset coach. As of September, I had landed three speaking engagements, two virtual summits and one podcast interview, for the remainder of 2020 and started my market research calls for my marketing business, which resulted in a number of individuals patiently anticipating the launch of my social media services because they would love to work with me already.

On October 2nd, after listening to my spirit and intuition versus going against the grain, I decided to put in my two weeks' notice for my full-time job because I wanted to be about the radical faith that I was talking about and seeking. I told myself that I was trusting God fully and that I was ready to jump into full-time entrepreneurship. All of the signs had been there, but I was letting fear and doubt cloud my mind and trouble my heart. I chose to let my faith be louder than my fears, notified my bosses of my decision, and moved accordingly.

In October, one of my supervisors for a contract position I am under at a black-owned marketing agency inquired about her being my first client under Moore Creative Media, as she is in the process of building three businesses for herself, to which I agreed! Under the other contract position I have, which is also a black-owned marketing agency, I am gradually moving into a leadership position of building their emerging Social Media department. My business coach has made a proposition to me about hosting a series of Masterclasses with her, as well as starting a sales coaching program that is scheduled to debut in November 2020, which also happens to be the same month that I would have relocated to a new environment. By November 1st, 2020, I am transitioning from Tuscaloosa, Alabama to Washington, D.C. The place I truly call home, seeing as I spent majority of my life there.

I will say, I did not expect God to move as quickly as he did. I didn't expect the blessings to come flooding in as strong as they have been, but I recognize the difference now. My prayers and conversations with God have become far more intentional than they have been before and despite my paradigm trying to project its fears and insecurities on my current reality, I truly believe everything that God has for me and I continue to operate in a mindset of abundance. I am learning to lean into God/my higher self more when it comes to my businesses and the decisions I make instead of being impulsive and only consulting with my flesh/ego. Gradually, I am learning that I can't operate these businesses without including God in the process.

Though writing new chapters can be nerve-wrecking, I can truly say that there is a level of inner peace that I feel in this new season of resilience and power. Turning my pain into purpose has been one of the most rewarding, peaceful feelings that I could ever experience. In the midst of the pain, it was so hard to see beyond the moment, but I am forever grateful for my gift of resilience and the ability to turn my adversity into accomplishments in all facets of my life.

About the Author:

Stephanie Moore, CEO & Founder of Moore Creative Media and Moore 2 Life Coaching + Wellness, is inspired by the one thing these two distinct niches of Marketing and Wellness have in common: helping individuals find their voice.

With four years, and counting, in the creative industry as a self-starter and a Bachelor of Social Work from the University of Alabama, Stephanie brings a duality of each niche that allows her to use analytical skills, conflict resolution, management/planning, and a plethora of other skills to help brands find a personable voice through passion and purpose, as well as within themselves!

Stay Connected with this Queen on social media:

Social Media:

Facebook: @MooreCreativeMedia

Instagram: @MooreCreativeMedia

CALLED BEYOND THE COMFORT ZONE

JESSIE JAMIAS

"When I called, you answered me; you made me bold and
courageous." — **Psalm 138:3**

I am an entrepreneur through and through. But haven't always been.

I used to dream about being "rich." I didn't even know what that
meant. All I knew was that I wanted my life to be different than what
I experienced growing up with my brother. We weren't poor. We had
everything we wanted. We were happy and my parents sacrificed a

lot for it. Dad worked shift work, which meant our time with him was inconsistent, quality time was seldom, and our relationship suffered as a result. Mom did what she could to find a job close to home so she could be present in our lives as much as possible. But I knew both parents didn't have their dream jobs, far from it. In fact, they didn't seem to chase dreams at all. Life wasn't about their success; it was about their family's well-being.

My brother and I were close in age, but not in our relationship. But sometimes we would brainstorm together about life as the rich and famous. We would become entrepreneurs, buy apartment buildings, and become landlords. And, of course, we would drive limousines. The things that young minds with big spirits would come up with. Sometimes we would make our stories extra ridiculous, although I had an unspoken belief that the ideas would never come to fruition.

As young children, we learned a lot from our parents. And one thing that followed me into my young adult life came from when I saw my parents work hard yet weren't completely happy. They were accepting of the life they were given. This developed into somewhat of a lack mindset for me, and I had a difficult time creating a vision for my life. I had a self-created belief that "dreaming" was meant to be a fun activity to think up outrageous ideas that would be hard or impossible to achieve, and would likely never transpire into anything.

For most of my life, I would make decisions which allowed me to stay within my comfort zone. I thought I was happy there because it led me to small wins, and achieving small goals consistently. I knew I would achieve a level of success in everything I did, although the level I envisioned wasn't high. I didn't have a faith in anything bigger than myself.

What I didn't realize is that those small goals were not pushing me to be a better person, and they were certainly not going to create any sort of impact on the world. Staying in my comfort zone was keeping me complacent, and not allowing me to stretch my mind, or find my passion. In fact, I spent years wondering if I would ever discover my passion.

I didn't always feel worthy around successful people. Being around them made me feel like I needed to prove myself, my worthiness and my abilities. It scared me. What if I didn't measure up? So I mostly kept my opinions and ideas to myself, and allowed others to take credit for my success. Although I was making strides in my life, none of those strides were significant because I wasn't working with intention. Every small action I was taking was leading me to a long, drawn-out version of a life which would be self-centered and not happy.

When I met my husband, I was working for a hotel company. Long hours and little pay. I was the youngest management in the company and earned myself little respect due to my young age. A boss once told me I was "just a girl getting by with looks and book smarts." The lack of respect made me feel insecure and emotionally closed. Although I worked hard, I had very low self-esteem and didn't feel worthy to have a good job and recognition. Looking back, I would tell my younger self to seek mentorship, people who could teach me to be stronger, to stand up for myself and to take what I earned because I deserved it.

My husband had always been an entrepreneur from a young age. He had made money from practically nothing and had built himself a really good reputation from his outgoing personality. He always tried to guide me into entrepreneurship and although it made me nervous, I did give it a try. My struggle was building relationships with people. I was so shy from past experiences. My self-doubt was falsely interpreted for snobbiness and it was difficult to gain new clients. I had a tiny voice inside of me that always wanted to be more. Determined to speak my voice, to become empowered and to change the world. But I allowed my introverted side to hold me back for years. I stayed well within my comfort zone and because of that, achieved only mediocre success in many areas of my life.

After years of putting in hard work for little results, I gave Network Marketing a try for the sole and only purpose of getting out of my comfort zone. I knew that I had a lot of work to do, if I was going to overcome my shyness, make my dreams come true, and inspire others to stand up for themselves. And to achieve this, I would have to spend time doing things that made me feel uncomfortable in a stretch-my-mind kind of way.

Network Marketing is what helped me to grow emotionally and allowed the potential I had inside of me to surface. Once I got used to talking to small crowds, I actually became really good at public speaking, and even started to enjoy it. And then I became pretty good at the business side, and teaching others. The company rewarded me with the use of a free car, diamond rings and a lot of cash bonuses.

After 5 years, I realized that something was missing. I was recruiting a lot of new women: really incredible, smart and talented women. I loved working with them. They became my sisters, my friends. But I felt like bringing these women into the network marketing field was like caging a beautiful bird. They had so much potential to change the world, to make a difference. I saw myself in them so profoundly. And just like me, they were stuck using their skills in a way that didn't allow them to make the huge impact they were destined to.

But the bigger piece that was missing was my faith. I had always believed that success was fully based on mindset and hard work. But what I failed to realize was that believing in something much bigger than myself was the true way to build upon the good things in life, and add value and unconditional love to the world.

I began to think of how I could still work with these incredible women, in a way that would allow me to empower them as much as I possibly could. I prayed about it, even when I didn't know how to pray. I believed there was so much more to this than what my own power could achieve. I wanted to love them in a way that allowed me to see every emotion, every passion, and every moment they held themselves back. I wanted to guide them to their pinnacle of success, by teaching them to use their voice, speak their truth and open their minds and hearts to believe that so much more was possible, even if they didn't see it for themselves.

I began to pray every day. I began to live my life with an open mind to allow possibility to flow. I would seek His presence continually and allow Him to guide my decisions. I believed wholeheartedly that every life I touched could be changed for the good with my words, and my actions. For the rest of the year, I vowed to say yes to every transformational opportunity that was presented. And my life began to finally unfold, in a powerful, emotional and momentous kind of way.

"It is the Lord who goes before you. He will be with you; He will guide you; He will not fail you or forsake you."

Women began to ask my opinion in business. Looking for guidance, suggestions, and input. Opportunities started to show up when I least expected and I started working closely with a couple friends who I knew were in jobs they didn't love. I knew they had dreams which they ignored. They had desires that were squished deep inside their hearts. And I was called to help them see the vision of what their life could look like, what their lifestyle could be if they were following their passion and actually getting paid to do something they loved.

This was the turning point for me. Watching them go from struggling or bored and complacent, to seeing the spark ignite inside their soul, the excitement begin to light up their face, their energy become more vibrant and happy. And to watch before my eyes the evolution in their presence. To see them grow from just thinking that God had a plan and they should remain status quo. To them understanding that God's plan was merely a guide to teach them lessons along the way, to open their way of thinking and allow them to grow in body, mind and spirit. The feeling inside me was that of sheer joy. A realization of why I was placed on this earth. From that moment, I had taken every one of God's lessons and rather than wondering why He had made me go through these obstacles in life, it was now so clear to me that each lesson was a stepping stone for me to learn and better understand people so I could use that gift to empower people to see their own gifts.

The cards each of us have been dealt, we have no control over. But when we are righteous, we will start to see that there are opportunities around us all day, every day and we can take our control back. We just have to be open enough to receive. As far as our energy goes, we have the ability to change our story. Instead of saying "I am so shy; I am an introvert," I now say "I spend every single day outside of my comfort zone; I attract like-minded people who want more for their life; I am completely energized and receive abundantly; people love joining me and I have the ability to change lives." What we tell ourselves over and over again will become our story.

So many of us have it backwards; we believe that once we achieve success, we will be happy. *Once I overcome my shyness I will be able to have more success.* But how it actually works is, we attract what we want by believing we already have it. By understanding that God has given us the ability to achieve it by consistently putting ourselves in that mindset every single day. Be the person you want to attract. Be the success that you are destined to be. Don't wait for it to come; take control and live like you already have it because you were called to live life outside of your comfort zone.

About the Author:

Jessie is a business coach, investor, serial entrepreneur and has built several online businesses. She has reached top positions in a former Network Marketing company and currently co-owns/manages a high-level entertainment company in her community. Jessie's mission is to ensure every income stream has a positive impact on people's lives.

Jessie is the founder/host of the *Unleash Your Confidence Show* and is known as an expert in personal evolution and turning something that was once a vision, into a tangible and lucrative business.

Stay Connected with this Queen on social media:

Instagram: instagram.com/jessiejamias

BRUISED, NOT BROKEN

NORMA REEVES

"He heals the broken-hearted and binds up their wounds." **Psalms 147:3**

How can God use me? I am a broken woman; I have been abused sexually, emotionally, physically, and spiritually; I was a single mother of 3 amazing boys. No one will ever take me seriously. How can I teach anyone how to reach their goals when I am struggling to believe my life matters?

Popularly called "The TAXLAYD," I am the founder and CEO of The Bottom Line Solutions. God called me to educate, equip, develop, and empower His people to go from becoming to BEING their own BOSS.

Growing up wasn't easy for me; by the age of 7, I had been sexually abused by my maternal grandfather and a maternal uncle by marriage. When I was nine, my mother was beaten brutally by her so-called boyfriend (beat her head against the concrete curb of the street because she was dancing with someone at a house party). She lay there for hours before any one assisted her, and when they did help her she was driven to the hospital and dropped off.

Doctors did not expect her to make it through the night, and if she did, she would not survive the brain surgery to reduce the swelling. However, God had a different plan. Although she did not die during surgery, parts of her died...her memory, her ability to speak, she was in a coma for 11 months. I spent every day at the hospital unable to visit her due to my age. When she was moved to a full-care facility, the first time I saw her there, there were tubes and beeping noises everywhere. As I stood there 10 years old, I could not comprehend what had happened to her. Out of nowhere, without warning, she began having seizures. What a scary sight for a little girl! She was 27 years old and remained there for the next 24 years until her accidental death at age 40.

I am the oldest of 4, but, unfortunately, I did not have the privilege and honor of growing up with all my brothers. My eldest brother and I were raised by our great mother (she was 75 when she took me in at birth). My third brother was born in prison and was immediately placed in foster care; we did get to spend time with him over the years until he was 7. My youngest brother was abandoned by my mother's friend whom she had left in her care. I remember the day they brought him to my grandmother's house so we could identify him. The courts would not allow my grandmother to take him due to her old age. So I watched them take my brother and I never saw him again. Both were eventually placed for adoption.

Do you know what it feels like to have 2 people out in the world with a connection to you, but you cannot connect? There has not been a day that I do not think about them; I do not feel complete with this void in my life and the hole in my heart.

I got pregnant at the age of 16, which was a very scary experience, but thank God my grandmother did not turn her back on me. Making the decision to have my baby would be one of the best decisions I made. I had a great support system; I was always an old soul, so my best friends were at least 10 years older than me; wisdom and compassion was plentiful.

I was impregnated by my best friend's brother. I remember when I told my grandmother we were getting married. Her exact words to me were: "Norma, that man is gonna take you away from me and beat your ass. He don't love you, girl." Needless to say I did not have her blessings or legal consent; however, I was going to marry this man in spite of everyone telling me not to, including his sisters. I tricked my mom into signing the consent form; I knew she did not know what she was doing.

We got married and two days later the beatings started, just like my grandmother said, (note to self – *you should listen when your elders are trying to warn you*) and continued for the next 5 years. He was a good provider for our son but a horrible husband and man. I lived in fear that if I told or left, he would kill me, just as he promised.

Excuses

There was a point during this period of time I remember praying out to God and begging Him to let me die quickly because I was tired of being beaten for the smallest of things. It took me being beaten to within an inch of my life in front of his father, grandfather, brother and my best friend before I would begin to be free .It was a feeling of deja vu, except it was me this time, not my mother. Because of the volume of blood loss, I passed out and was rushed to the hospital via ambulance. I would spend 21 days in the hospital having reconstructive surgeries and protective care with guards around my room. The guards were volunteers from his softball league; they took turns making sure he did not get a chance to finish what he started.

I will forever be grateful and thankful to my best friend for standing up to all those men who watched from afar. She forced me to tell my father and uncles (they did not do a lot of taking-names first); however, the stakes were high, as I did not want them to kill him and spend the rest of their lives in prison. So I decided to go to the police; I knew this could mean death for me, but God intervened.

I was afraid to live, as the fear of retaliation was crippling. I had no confidence, no self-esteem, no hopes. No dreams of a future lived without fear.

Run to Live

I awoke one morning and thought about how miserable my life was. With $26 in my pocket, I caught a ride with one of my father's friends and left the place I had called home. I made my way to Florida where my mom's best friend, my auntie, lived.

For the first time in forever, I felt safe. I guess if God was going to fix me He needed me to be somewhere warm and away from everyone that had ever hurt me. He was the surgeon; I was the patient. I was on the Surgeon's table and I refused to get up before time. Little by little, I began to dream and see my future.

In the meantime, my baby was with his father. How could I leave my baby? Well, it was hard, but when you are running for your life, you have to leave certain people and things. You see, this man had used my son against me; he told me that if I wanted him, I had to come back to him. Leaving my son was the second hardest choice I made. Remember I said he was a good dad and provider to our son, so I knew he would take good care of him, but it did not change the fact that, as a mother, I wasn't supposed to leave my baby. I know what abandonment feels like and I promised myself I would keep my children, no matter what. I told myself "this is not permanent" and kept my word.

Three months later, I was ready to rescue my son. The plan was in play. I traveled back to the place where I experienced my darkest moments; however, this time, I was in control. With the help of my best friend, I got my son back and nothing would separate us again.

Yes, I snuck into his father's house, grabbed my baby, and ran for my life to my bestie's awaiting car…. Together again.

It was time I stopped making excuses; God had a plan and purpose for my life. I was not dead and fear was behind me. God had surrounded me with powerful women who would not give up on me or allow me to give up on myself.

If you are reading this, know this: you are right where you need to be. Now is the time for you to shake off the shackles of self-doubt. Stand up straight, look yourself in the eye, and tell yourself, "Today is the day I choose to walk out and SNATCH my life back. Do you know how many people are depending on you to succeed? You hold the key to someone's freedom. No one ever said it would be easy. The truth is that anything worth having must be fought for; you have to fight like your life depends on it.

Close your eyes and picture the hands of God; everything you are dealing with has been filtered through His powerful hands. You are stronger than you think; you just have to see yourself positioned, seated in your Royal throne.

About the Author:

Norma is a self-proclaimed serial "get out your rut" motivational speaker married to her soulmate, mother of 4 adult sons, and 1 beautiful daughter. Her greatest title is SWEETIE, the name her 8 grand babies bestowed on her.

She has helped hundreds of small business owners go from barely making it to now running multimillion dollar enterprises. No dream is too small; no bank account is too small. All you need is a dream.

She has a passion for helping women in abusive relationships find their voice and the courage to take back what was stolen –their dignity.

Stay Connected with this Queen on Social Media:

Twitter: bruisednotbroken

IG: thenormareeves

Thenormareeves.com

Bruisedbutotbroken.com

Help@thenormareeves.com

PIVOT. POSITION. PROSPER!

TINA D. LEWIS

"…they that wait upon the Lord will renew their strength. They will soar on wings like eagles; they will run and not be weary, they will walk and not be faint" **(Isaiah 40:31).**

2020 is my year!

Well, that's what I proclaimed! I and many others I know. We even had vision boards and girl gatherings in 2019 to discuss exactly how it was going to go. I knew If I did exactly what I did for my clients and for myself last year, with just a few minor tweaks, less procrastination and firing on all cylinders #allgasnobrakes, this year would be a piece of cake! My goal was to earn 1 Million dollars, author 10 books, help more of my clients become bestselling authors, mentor 20 clients to $100k in 180 days, launch 3 new revenue-generating platforms, invest in real estate, travel to Croatia, Paris, and Dubai, just to name a few. I had BHAG (Big Hairy Audacious Goals)! You think??

As I returned from a Social Media conference that was held in the beautiful ocean-lined city of San Diego, California, I heard rumors of a virus and the possible ban on travel. ABSURD! There go those conspiracy theorists again! ☺

NEWSFLASH: *March 13, 2020: President Donald Trump declares a U.S. national emergency, and on March 15th, the CDC warns against large gatherings of 50 or more.*

WAIT! I'm THE Bottomline Strategist. I multiply the revenue and profits of entrepreneurs and small business owners! I Mentor, Coach, Train, Teach, Speak, Network, Brunch, Dinner and duhhhh... GATHER for a living! ☺

I must admit, initially, I was devastated but remained hopeful. "This shouldn't last for more than a few weeks," I thought. However, 48 hours later on March 17th: the virus was present in all 50 states and every day there were new discoveries and even more restrictions. As if things couldn't get any worse, on March 19th, the Governor of California issued a Statewide Stay-at-Home Order mandating all residents to stay at home except to go to an essential job (that they defined) or shop for essential needs. REALLY! Didn't I tell you that I am THE Bottomline Strategist and I MUST gather and travel?!

Even though I was frustrated and in disbelief, I remembered a billionaire mentor of mine saying, "Tina, if you want to become wealthy, find out where the world is going and get there during the first wave. You don't have to be first, just get there. When you do that, you will never have to worry about money again! Simply BE the solution to a need!"

Unconsciously, I did just that!

PIVOT: I was invited to a Zoom conference call hosted by a top nephrologist who called on community leaders, influencers, healthcare providers, pastors, and anyone who had an interest in purveying the proper education and information to the communities in need. I have a genuine concern and compassion for people and am trained as a Physician Assistant, so I was "in the room!" I wanted to donate my services in any capacity (because I'm no longer licensed, I can't administer drugs, write prescriptions or perform surgery, but I was willing to do whatever it took)! On approximately our third call, one of the administrators of a medical clinic stated that they and other clinics were in need of masks and other medical supplies. I went from listening intently as a participant to interrupting the conversation, as a moderator requesting his contact information, assuring him that I could fulfill the order and would call him afterward. Under normal circumstances, I would say, I have no idea "why" or "where" that came from, but as a Faith walker, I simply trusted God.

In the midst of the "pandemic" and all the new discoveries about the virus, physicians, first responders, healthcare workers and the American people felt scared and unsafe. Protective gear such as masks, gloves, eye gear, facial protective shields, hand sanitizer, alcohol pads, surgical gowns and many other medical supplies were extremely scarce and in high demand. No one expected a pandemic, so stocks were insufficient and no shipments from overseas were admitted into the United States (especially China because that was where the "virus" was said to have originated).

POSITION: We did some research, made a few phone calls, and by the grace of God, Protective Gear Unlimited was birthed! It was a challenge to procure the merchandise, but we prevailed. We had masks, gloves, face shields and gowns.

June 2020, the number of people who had contracted the virus reached 2 million! Our economy remained strained and shut down as 22 million Americans were unemployed. (Praise Break) In the midst of a pandemic, I was able to position myself and my business to thrive. With just two orders from the clinics, more than half of my year's income was replaced. HALLELUJAH!

As the world began to accept that wearing masks, facial protective clothing, working from home and virtual meetups were the norm, many entrepreneurs and business owners realized they needed to pivot. Mastering strategies, blueprints, launches, webinars and collaborations to replace the lost income first and then supersede that, was a priority. There is nothing like having the expertise and skillset to build a system that would provide CPR to a financially choking entity! It's my superpower!

Protective Gear Unlimited was fresh, new, and extremely profitable, but it wasn't my passion. It didn't make me want to "get up and get at it!" It was simply God throwing me a life jacket because He saw that I was getting ready to drown like so many of my friends, family, clients, colleagues and the American people.

PROSPER: You see, I had made my plans, written them in ink, and was ready to execute, but God prepared something different, just like He says: (Jeremiah 29:11) "'For I know the plans I have for you,' declares the LORD, 'plans to prosper you and not to harm you, plans to give you hope and a future.'" Not only did He have a ram in the bush to carry me through turbulent times, He also provided a vehicle where I earned almost $50,000 ($47,812 to be exact) in 60 days. That's not even the best part. I was also able to help my friends and clients earn some income too! Yes! During an economic debacle! (Praise dance and shuffle right here!)

This is just a glimpse of how God shows up and conspires the universe to move on our behalf. He has and will always operate as such in our lives. We just simply have to be available for the prompting. I say this now but it didn't always come to me this way. I was distracted trying to survive as a single, teenage mother on welfare, living in the projects, dodging drugs, gangs and even bullets . . . literally! Let's just say, God has protected me and kept me. Why am I sharing this? Because I don't want you to see my glory without my story! That's my GPS. It shows me where I came from, keeps me going in the right direction and U turns are prohibited.

It's been FULL STEAM AHEAD. Even though I'm trained as a health care professional, a PA, I discovered very early on that I was chronically unemployable. I worked at a clinic located in Watts, CA and was honored to have the exposure. While working there, I started a housekeeping service which was my first taste of entrepreneurship. I was smitten and have had numerous businesses ever since. Some were a bust, others were profitable, and the latter ones were explosive! I guess things do get better with time or shall I say "experience and results!"

I have a gift and I don't take it for granted: I can take any business model, from a lemonade stand, a makeup artist, a teacher, a nurse, a speaker, an author, a printing shop to a Fortune 100, 500 or 5000 company and drastically multiply their revenue and profit margin (if I can't create a blueprint or strategy to enhance your bottom line, then there is none). I've been called the "Cash Flow Catalyst" by the Small Business Expo, the Queen of Rapport & Recruiting, an Expert and even a Magician. As long as the results are substantiated, I'll take it!

I know it's uncomfortable in this season. You may be terrified or maybe you're thriving. The bottom line is, where do you go from here? If you don't know, let me tell you! UP! No matter where you are, where you've been, the direction is up! That's the only way you'll be able to take your rightful position, Queen.

You are fearfully and wonderfully made. (Psalms 139:14). A royal priesthood (I Peter 2:9). You're the head and not the tail, above and not beneath, the lender and not the borrower. You matter. You are enough and everything you need to operate in royalty is already within you! Do you know why you have those unbelievable dreams and crazy, outlandish ideas? Take one guess! Because God not only gave them to you, but He's equipped you with exactly what you need to fulfill that assignment as well.

Bottom line: Queen, it's time to Pivot. What do you REALLY want? What do you enjoy doing? And what impact are you desiring to make? Position yourself to be used as a witness, to bring hope to others and position yourself as an authority in your life and/or your business. Joshua 1:8,9 says: "This book of the law shall not depart from thy mouth; but thou shall meditate in it day and night, that you may observe to do according to all that is written therein: for then, you shall make thy way prosperous, and then you shalt have good success."

I'm a Faith walker. Are you? Grab my hand, Queen. It's time to Pivot. Position and Prosper!

About the Author:

Tina D. Lewis is a keynote speaker, bestselling author, master trainer and philanthropist. She is known as The Bottomline Strategist. Tina's keen sense of Math, Marketing and Business acumen is unparalleled! She multiplies revenues and profits of entrepreneurs and small business owners. How can I help? What's your bottom line??

Stay Connected with this Queen on Social Media:

FB & IG - @tinadlewis

Phone: 323.239.1362

Email: info@TinaDLewis.com

"I WAS THE WEAPON FORMED AGAINST MYSELF THAT PROSPERED!"

EBONY WALKER

"No weapon formed against thee shall prosper; and every tongue that shall rise against thee in judgment thou shalt condemn. This is the heritage of the servants of the Lord, and their righteousness is of Me, saith the Lord." **- Isaiah 54:17 (KJV)**

Wife. Mother. Daughter. Sister. Pastor. Entrepreneur. Mentor. Woman.

Many of us operate in these titles without blinking an eye. Day by day, it's like clockwork. We do what's necessary daily to thrive, survive, and stay alive. But the unfortunate truth is that in the midst of all of those titles we carry and all the hats we wear, we often leave off one vital description: *weapon*!

Yes, weapon. Yes, an instrument or device used to attack. Yes, an object used against an opponent. And while it sounds comical to think of "weapon" as being one of our many titles, that's exactly what we are 90% of our lives. Then again, maybe it's just me...

I'm a Believer in Jesus Christ. No, I don't know EVERY single scripture in the Bible, but I've learned a great deal of them. Yet, it amazes me how I became so great at quoting scriptures and applying them to the lives of everyone else; but, when it came to me, I fell short. My faith wasn't up to par and I didn't believe that "better" could find me. I surely didn't have that mustard seed faith that would allow "it" – whatever "it" was – to work for my good. I was able to preach and teach hope, healing, restoration, and transformation to everybody else – but I failed to do it to myself. And, one day, this caused me to recognize a very harsh truth. I, in fact, had become the weapon, formed against myself, that prospered!

Isaiah 54:17 (KJV) states it so clearly: *No weapon formed against thee shall prosper; and every tongue that shall rise against thee in judgment thou shalt condemn. This is the heritage of the servants of the Lord, and their righteousness is of Me, saith the Lord.*

I believed that I was a servant of God. But how is it possible to serve God AND fear simultaneously? How is it possible to serve God AND be double-minded? Somehow, I'd mastered it and didn't even know it! I was going to bed late, praying for others. I was waking up in the wee hours of the morning, encouraging others. I was trying to get my husband to believe that God would heal him. I was trying to raise my child in the way he should go. I was fasting for God to work miracles in the lives of loved ones and church family. But guess what? I didn't have sense enough to fast and pray for myself.

I found myself living in the lies of my past and the opinions of others. I had become blanketed between false expectations and damaging word curses. I even attached depression to my right side and lack to my left hip – all because it was comfortable and familiar. It was whom I'd been for so long. It's sad how we can become so used to being on the bottom shelf that we don't strive for anything higher; yet, we blame our circumstances for our inability to rise. But usually, WE are in the way 100% of the time and WE block our climb while choosing to fault others.

I was operating in doubt and defeat. I was angry at the lack that I'd welcomed, which wouldn't leave. I even talked myself out of major opportunities. Yes, these were the conversations I had with myself. And somewhere along the line, I chose to believe that the weapons formed against me were only from outward forces. And it became synchronic to denounce and cast down *those* weapons. I had no problem decreeing and declaring *those* issues to be powerless. However, it didn't dawn on me that every weapon attempting to take me out – be it physically, mentally, emotionally, or spiritually – wasn't always from "the enemy." Most came from *the inner me*! And therein arose the greatest epiphany of my life: I had mastered becoming a weapon against myself! That became a title, a badge of honor, in the worst way.

I thought I was being humble. I was actually afraid to accept that there was a royal position I belonged in. And because my excuses had become my dwelling place, I found myself out of line and out of position. I couldn't believe it! I'd let the lies about me, which I'd chosen to believe, take my spot!

It's synonymous with having an assigned seat at a major event. Let's say, for instance, the Grammy's. Before the guests arrive, you see sheets of paper with names on them. Every star has their name on a seat throughout the theatre. And guess what? They don't apologize for it. Why? Because they've worked hard to get where they are and are unregretful about their accomplishments. If their position is on "Row 2/Seat 4," that's where they'll sit. Point blank. But for us, it's a different story. We've become a generation that accepts seat fillers. Seat fillers are people who *have* to take the position of the ones who didn't show up, like a substitute.

One day, I looked through the chapters of my life and realized that I had given up my position far too many times. I was afraid to fire my seat filler because I was more concerned with who would approve me sitting in my seat. But if I'm supposed to be prosperous, if I'm supposed to be royalty, how dare I allow someone else to take my spot? If the seat has my name and DNA on it, why would I so willingly give it up?

I had to rebuke myself. I know we don't do that too often. But it's necessary. I had to look myself in the mirror and say, "Girl, quit trippin'!" Having a mirror experience is something we should all do. It'll make you aware of the layers that you've put on, pretending to have it all together. And my layers included my husband falling ill, our financial rut, keeping ministry afloat, being a caretaker, raising our teenaged son, and so much more. Day by day, I ignored the layers by staying busy. I made myself believe that doing all the "necessary stuff" meant that I was pleasing God. However, there's nothing worse than doing "good" things, but forgetting the "God" things. And that's where I was.

I was being a good person, but I wasn't being an obedient one. I believed that if I "worked" and had faith, He'd make it better. I'd taken the "faith without works is dead" scripture to a whole new level, but was STILL doing it wrong. And in the midst of my "busy-ness," God kept reminding me that my gift would make room for me, BUT I had to make room for Him and obey.

I had to step out on faith and start my business. But in doing so, I had to eliminate the art of blaming those who rejected me and focus on the real issue: why did I leave God? We don't often like to admit that our ways of doing things are often the farthest from what God requires. He has literally given us EVERYTHING that pertains to life and godliness; yet, we seem to add our ingredients to the recipe. Then we get an attitude because it doesn't taste right! But I was tired of eating this disgusting gumbo that I'd created. It tasted horrible and never filled me up. Therefore, I changed up my recipe for His!

First, I had to commit to His agenda and relinquish my own. After all, He's the Author and Finisher so who was I to attempt penning my steps in His plan?

Next, I had to be ok with taking risks. And, yes, that was even the ones that "man" didn't agree with or understand. If God instructed me, compliance was necessary!

Third, eliminating beliefs had to be released. Too many things were mentally holding me back and staking claim to my greatness. Stinking thinking HAD to go!

Fourth, I had to stop settling for temporary happiness and pursue joy. Joy comes, even in the midst of darkness. And without joy, we thrive off of mere emotions – which are as stable as the wind.

Fifth, I had to embrace that I was graced with powerful gifts and talents. And I was not allowed to apologize for having them. The wealth and resources that were waiting on me could only find me when I stepped into the grace that I was given to operate therein.

Lastly, I had to recognize my value. Putting myself on a shelf in the pawnshop was no longer acceptable. The real appraisal came through the Word of God, not the words of man, and definitely not the lies of myself.

I was always told, as a child, that I would never amount to anything. Because of the choices my parents made, I was coined to be the next negative statistic. Family members, old and young, would taunt me and tell me I'd end up on drugs. They'd tell me I was destined to be a failure. One even told me to just give up and sleep around because releasing my body to strangers would be all I'd ever be great at. And, for years, I held on to that. As a teenager, I was confused about who I needed to become. I knew what I didn't want, but I began to settle for it – thinking that I had no other choice.

Shame on me.

I had to learn that it's never really about "them" or what "they" did. It's never about "their" perception. It's more so about what I believe, concerning me, and how I have to consciously shift the dynamics of my own thought processes – ensuring that they align with the Word of God.

If you're reading this, I need you to know that hanging on to excuses is no longer optional or accepted. Whoever it was that said whatever they said, they're irrelevant. They're jesters. They're peasants. And they should not be allowed to continue stunting your growth.

Your royal position is just that – YOUR position!

I made a choice to grab mine. I didn't want seat fillers warming up the spot where I belonged. I can warm up my own spot! But that couldn't happen until I stopped turning the gun on myself, until I stopped lying about the way I was feeling, and until I stopped sleeping with the lack that had become comfortable.

When I stopped turning the gun on myself, all things became new. And it was at that moment that I realized the definitiveness of Romans 8:28 (KJV):

And we know that all things work together for good to them that love God, to them who are the called according to His purpose.

Yes, and NOW I KNOW – ALL things work! Therefore, I'm laying down my weapon so that I can be a part of His wedding. When the Bridegroom comes, I have to show that I followed Him and not the lies I told myself. He's expecting me to present myself without spot or wrinkle, and I have to iron out the kinks and foolery now.

That's what the mindset of royalty will do. And now, I can turn those weapons in the right direction. No more excuses, no more entertaining foul verbiage, but only hearing and adhering to what the Father says.

About the Author:

Ebony Walker is a North Carolina native and the Owner of *Walk UpWrite*. She has made a powerful and professional name for herself as a copywriter, ghostwriter, author, speaker, and preacher of the Gospel. She currently resides in Fayetteville, NC with her husband, Apostle John Walker. Collectively, they have 4 children, 7 grandchildren, and 1 special goddaughter.

Her favorite verse is Romans 8:28 – *because all things TRULY work for the good.*

Stay Connected with this Queen on Social Media:

Visit https://linktr.ee/ebonywalker

FROM TRAUMA TO TROPHIES

CHERISH P. JACKSON

"Even so faith, if it hath not works, is dead, *being* alone"
(James 2:17 KJV).

The air was stiff while my body trembled with each exhale. I closed the closet door and fell to my knees, feeling lost and drained. I was sure the decision to end my life was for certain. I had attempted suicide once before in 2011. My breath was short as my lungs were closing up. My eyes clouded with tears while my right hand filled with pills. I screamed at God, "You said you wouldn't put too much on me that I couldn't handle; God, why this? You only test Your strongest soldiers. I'm not that strong!" At that moment, it was clear I was closed out of God's life. My holy trinity consisted of *me, failures, and trauma*. I shuffled the pills in my hand and tossed them in my mouth. My saliva became thick from the powder-based capsules. I hesitated before taking a big gulp. At that moment, I cared about no one. In the end, I vomited and became ill. God had spared me once more from my attempts.

Transparently, I attempted suicide once more after this. It was not nearly as detrimental as the first and second attempt, yet still significant. My memoir could fill as many pages as the Bible. I have undergone almost every trauma imaginable. I have been traumatized by sexual abuse to domestic violence. I will disclose, there are other traumas in between those listed that would cause for more pages and more therapy.

I grew up in Chicago, Illinois, 25th/Washtenaw. My community had violence, poverty, and a lack of ambition. Murders were common in the surrounding areas, and some of my close friends were indebted to gang affiliations. One thing I can say we thrived on was charisma. We had very little, but we still held school plays, assemblies, Halloween parties, and birthday celebrations. Sometimes local churches would gather funds to purchase Christmas presents for families in need. I loved writing my Christmas letter to Santa each year. I remember my mother took us all to pick up gifts. We stood in line for close to an hour in the cold. Snow filled our socks, but the joy of love filled our hearts.

Graciously, my family sacrificed to make sure we had what we needed. I do not glorify overworking or overexhausting yourself. I do glorify the phrase, "Even so faith, if it hath not works, is dead, *being alone*" (James 2:17 King James Version). In other words, you have to put in the work *(natural)* for God to give you the blessing *(super)*. There, you will find a *supernatural blessing.* Just praying will not suffice. Just praying did not allow Jesus to minister and save thousands of lives; He had to put in the natural work. He had to walk, sweat, cry, and persevere. God wants the same for us. My attempts did not come to fruition because I had not adjusted my crown to see the beauty in my queendom.

Ultimately, past residue from trauma was living in the crevices of my heart and soul. I was unhappy my crown had fallen from my head. My agony was my excuse to attempt suicide. My journey to mental wellness started at the age of 19. I knew I had asthma, but did not discover I had other health conditions that provided discomfort to my mental stability. As a child, I would tap things a certain amount of times until I found mental relief. In sixth grade, I split my middle finger open, down to the bone, on a light bulb. I did not understand why I had to tap and squeeze things three times. I picked up the light bulb, squeezed and tapped it once. I squeezed it and tapped it twice. On the last tap, the glass ruptured my finger, piercing my skin and jetting blood all over the walls. Blood flew from my finger like a water gun. At 19, I was diagnosed with Obsessive-Compulsive Disorder. I was happy to know there was a name for what I was experiencing.

My other two disorders are Severe Anxiety Disorder: Panic Attacks, and Psychophysiological Insomnia. My journey with Severe Anxiety is coarse. When I become anxious, I hemorrhage, faint, tic involuntarily, or have panic attacks. I was diagnosed with Psychophysiological Insomnia at the age of 25. I get around 4 hours of sleep a night. I wake up from night terrors and/or sleep paralysis. Daily, I feel mentally drained from anxiety, compulsions, and lack of sleep.

Forward, I know you are wondering what made me drop my excuses to play my royal position in faith, personal life, and career. I used to let my trials dictate my mood. I used to let my traumas and past experiences be my path maker. The only path maker and way maker is Christ. God will break you down to rebuild pieces of you. We may have strength, but the backbone of that strength often comes from fear of betrayal. We may have compassion, but the backbone of that compassion often comes from the fear of abandonment. God has to break us free from the backbone of our core beliefs and rebuild us for the better.

I prided myself on being a strong Black Woman. I admired everything about the aspect of a strong Black Woman. God had to break me of that ill mentality. I was only strong because I was suppressing pain. I was only strong because I had not dealt with the residue of my past traumas. Once I started uncovering it all, the odor of toxicity smothered the room. A lot of things in my life had a reeking smell that needed spiritual cleansing and therapy. I dropped my excuses because God allowed me to live after three suicide attempts. People are living with mental health disorders that have not discovered their calling. Some Black women have faced a multitude of traumatic experiences that need a haven. These core reasons keep my vision alive. I had to use my mess as a message for God's people.

From a bright perspective, I am the founder of Orange Daisies, LLC, a mental health and bath company established on May 18, 2020. My vision is to bless those who are mentally unwell through hydrotherapy and mental health techniques we can store in our toolbox. When we feel discomfort, it could spiral into a deep depression due to the lack of tools in our toolbox. Mental health disorders are real, and so is mental unwellness. I believe in Jesus and therapy. Praying will get you far, but tools such as mindfulness meditations can assist in your overall betterment too.

Likewise, being an entrepreneur while having a full-time career is challenging. I face many obstacles such as beating the social media algorithm, implementing new content, posting content frequently to social media, all while giving one hundred percent to my students. As a Special Education teacher in a moderate-to-severe Autism unit, self-contained (I have them for all subjects. I am their homeroom teacher), while working with nonverbal students, is exhausting. My students are from 3rd-5th grade. I lesson plan for various abilities while making sure my business does not plummet. I host parent-teacher conferences all while doing live interviews on social media regarding mental health.

Although wearing the hat of a full-time entrepreneur and full-time career professional is exhilarating, I work in a career field I love, dedicate mental wellness techniques to my sorority Sigma Gamma Rho, Inc., and help thousands of Strivers reach their optimal wellness. I may not be rich in the flesh, but before the Lord I am wealthy. I turned my trauma into trophies. Remember, the very thing you feel ashamed about could very well be an avenue for greatness.

Meanwhile, allow me to tell you my secrets to success in being a full-time entrepreneur and full-time career professional:

- Attend free webinars
- Dedicate specific days for only business and only career
- Put your work down after 6 pm
- Host free training/webinars to grow your email list for marketing
- First career, life second, business third; if you are going to remain a full-time career professional and entrepreneur
- Be honest in the work you present
- Know that growth takes time
- If it feels off, it *is* off. Trust your gut when it comes to business deals
- Make pillars for your company and live by them
- Do not volunteer for extra duties at work if you know that will subtract from home life

As I newly invest in entrepreneurship, these concepts have guided me to a simplistic outlook. I have learned so much from free webinars. It is free information that trades your time for knowledge. In your business, be transparent, honest, and fair.

Respectfully, I want to close by wishing you well. Your crown will fall many times. You will be unsuccessful, and people will take advantage of you. The beauty in it all is that you can use your pain as a pillar. Joy is in the journey of our failures. Take note that success is not measured on if we win or lose. Success is relevant to exposure and experience. Use the trials as pressure and persistence. I also want you to seek help, Queen. Clean up all the dirty things lingering in your spirit and personality. You are brilliant, passionate, bold, and a victorious Striver!

About the Author:

Cherish P. Jackson is a Special Education teacher. She serves as the owner of Orange Daisies, LLC, a mental health and bath company. Her company's tenets are to educate others on mental health disorders, provide mental wellness skills for your toolbox, and provide various ways to strive towards wellness through hydrotherapy.

Stay Connected with this Queen:

Social media handles & Website:

Website: www.orangedaisiesblog.com

Instagram @orangedaisiesllc

Facebook: @orangedaisiesllc

Facebook Group: Orange Daisies Social Group

QUEEN, HERE'S YOUR CHANCE

If you have read this book in its entirety and you are ready to Play Your Royal Position in the Body of Christ but are not quite sure how, I invite you to get to know a man named Jesus through the salvation prayer!

*Dear **Lord** Jesus, I know that I am a sinner, and I ask for Your forgiveness. I believe that You are the Son of God and alone You died for my sins and rose again on the third day to give me life! I willingly turn from my sins and invite You to come into my heart and life. I will trust and follow You as my **Lord** and Savior from this day forward. I believe that I am a New Creature in YOU!*

In Jesus Name I pray…

AMEN!

Queen, I believe that if you prayed that prayer aloud in spirit and in truth, then you are now a TRUE Queen in the Body of Christ. You are a New Creature and the former you is gone. I want to encourage you to get into a good bible-based church, community, or virtual environment to help you continue on this journey in support and love.

I'd love to hear your story! Please email us at: info@jesuscoffeeandprayer.com In the subject line, please put: SAVED

I personally want to welcome you into the body of
Christ and as my Sister!

You have taken the Ultimate step to Playing Your Royal
Position and I am Proud of YOU!
Love You to LIFE!

Min. Nakita Davis
CEO & Founder of Jesus Coffee and Prayer Christian
Publishing House LLC.
www.jesuscoffeeandpayer.com

SPECIAL THANKS

Queen Sponsors

Thank You, Frances Jones, M.A

On behalf of Jesus, Coffee, and Prayer Christian Publishing House LLC, we would like to thank you for believing in this Movement, Dream, and Vision! May God bless you richly in ALL that you touch!

Frances Jones holds master's degrees from the University of Mississippi in accounting and educational leadership. She is a certified professional coach, Energy Leadership Index master practitioner, and the founder of Heart Desires Fulfillment Coaching,

LLC. She specializes in infertility coaching and has more than twenty years of personal infertility experience.

She uses her story and the empowering lessons she learned to inspire, motivate, encourage, and help others who are dealing with negative emotions and stigmas associated with fertility challenges.

Frances lives in Memphis, Tennessee, with her family.

2020 WOMEN OF INFLUENCE HONOREES

"A Woman of Influence is a Queen who uses her gifts, position, and affluence to help other Queens Rise up to Play their Own Royal Position. She recognizes her God-given power yet moves with *Grace.* She adds value to every room she enters and leads NOT with the intent to create more followers; but with the intent to ***create more LEADERS***!

She is a Woman of Influence" ~ Min. Nakita Davis

DR. CHERLY WOOD

Women of Influence~ All-Star

VOCALIZE Women Speakers Academy

Dr. Cheryl Wood is the CEO of VOCALIZE Women Speakers Academy, an International empowerment and TEDx Speaker. She is a 12x best-selling author and master speaker development coach who equips entrepreneurs with the tools to unleash the power of their voice and transform other people's lives with their story. Dr. Wood has trained countless leaders across the United States and abroad in South Africa, India, France, United Kingdom, Canada and the Bahamas to face their fears, get out of their comfort zone, take calculated risks, and pursue their big dreams.

She has been featured on ABC, Radio One, Forbes Magazine, Huffington Post, ESSENCE, Black Enterprise, Rolling Out, Sheen

Magazine, Good Morning Washington, Fox 5 News, Fox 45 News, The Washington Informer, The Baltimore Times, Afro-American Newspaper and has delivered riveting keynote presentations for organizations including NASA, The United Nations, the FBI, Verizon, and United States Department of Defense.

Follow this Queen:

http://facebook.com/groups/impactnationwen

http://instagram.com/cherylempowers

http://cherylempowers.com

NIKKI RICH

Women of Influence ~All-Star

The Nikki Rich Show

Nikki Rich is the CEO of *The Nikki Rich Show* in LA, California. She is an Oprah Winfrey Network Ambassador/OWN Media & Press •Toyota Rav 4 Series Fresh Perspectives Radio Host •2x Amazon International Best-Selling Author •3x Amazon Best-Selling Author •For(bes) The Culture Member •2 Seasons NYFW HITechModa (plus) Runway Model •Contributor for TMZ/Corresponding •6x Featured Cover Magazine •6 National Billboards Los Angeles CA, Memphis TN , Hawthorne CA, Atlanta GA Broadcasting Network •The Nikki Rich Show - Cable TV spectrum ch 32 AT&T Uverse ch 99 •Podcast - Iheart Radio & Apple.

Follow this Queen:

Instagram/Twitter: @NikkiRichShowtv

FB: The Nikki Rich Show Website TheNikkiRichShow.com

TIFFANY D. BELL

Women of Influence

Leading with Uncommon Courage

As a CEO of a nonprofit, an author, entrepreneur, coach, mother, and friend - my goal is to inspire, empower, and equip women to make positive, life-giving choices for themselves and others. My calling in life is to connect people to resources, people to people, and most importantly - people to God!

Bio: Tiffany Denise Bell is a nonprofit consultant, coach, author, and speaker. She is not only co-director of Success Women's Conference, but she is also the founder of Uncommon Courage, a platform created to inspire and equip women to find, embrace, and connect with their unique voice and purpose with confidence.

As a nonprofit leader, she has over 25 years of experience in community outreach and leadership training.

Follow this Queen:

https://www.facebook.com/UnCommonCourage.cc/

https://www.instagram.com/uncommon_courage/

MICHELLE THOMAS

Women of Influence

UnSPOKEN: Real Talk of Today's Blended Family

I am a Woman of Influence because I have a lifetime of adversities that SHOULD have defeated me, but it MADE ME! My personal mantra is that LIFE is my "Unframeable Degree!" Where man discounted my abilities because I did not learn what I know from a textbook, GOD blessed me with the wisdom, discernment, and knowledge strictly built for His purpose for me: helping people! I, openly and confidently, share my story – the good, bad, and ugly – with my audience so they can KNOW that they deserve Health, Happiness, Peace, and Love.

Bio: I am a Wife, Mother, Author, Motivational Speaker, Coach, and Minority Business Owner. I have 7 children – 6 boys and 1 girl – and we are a blended family. I am the author of unSPOKEN Real Talk of Today's Blended Family. I also own a hair company, a design company, a publishing company, and my husband and I own a Corporate Parent Company.

Follow this Queen:

https://facebook.com/authormichelle.thomas

https://www.instagram.com/healthylove_michellesthomas

RAVEN WILLIAMS

Women of Influence

Author/Speaker

Creating opportunities that will positively impact our generation and lay a foundation for future generations are very important to me. Through inspirational conversations, books, and live sessions, I work to creatively inspire and influence others to embrace their purpose and believe that they've already won.

Bio:

Raven J Williams is a highly motivated speaker, author, leader, and businesswoman who empowers her audiences to believe in themselves with her energetic and thought-provoking approach to pushing past obstacles and succeeding. Raven is also the Founder of Blueprint Coaching Solutions, LLC, where she coaches, mentors, and creates a working strategy for individuals and non-profit leaders to prepare, implement, and excel in their personal life, in business, and in the community. Her unique approach to helping to shift the mindset of those whom she encounters and help them find their purpose is based on her personal mission tagline: "Transforming you, One Conversation at a Time."

Follow this Queen:

FB & IG: @ravenjwilliams

DR. JENNIFER BRYANT

Women of Influence

Reaching Within, An Empowerment Journey

As a Woman of Influence, I impact lives and have been recognized for my impact in my community, leadership skills, and devotion to mentoring and elevating women's careers and enhancing professional development. I've been commended for my hard work, commitment, and contributions to serving and enriching communities, and the world.

Bio:

Dr. Jennifer Jones Bryant is the Executive Founder of Reaching Within, An Empowerment Journey LLC, Best-Selling Author,

Award-Winning Certified Life Coach, Career Strategist, Mentor, Adjunct Instructor, Global Speaker, Retired Federal Senior Executive, and Podcast Host. She has over 31 years of demonstrated expertise helping individuals and teams in the federal government and corporate become high performers and more marketable to accelerate their careers through her leadership.

As a best-selling author and speaker, she regularly receives speaking invitations from federal agencies, academia, and community organizations. She has been featured in Speakers Magazine, Faith Heart, Glam CEO, Power 20, Women on the Verge, VoyATL, One Tribe, and UpWord global magazines, the Washington Post, Making Headlines News, Radio One, Great Day Washington WUSA, ThatAnitaLiveShow, and numerous Podcast interviews.

Follow this Queen:

FB:
https://www.facebook.com/groups/235666466973279/?ref=share

IG: Https://www.instagram.com/ReachingWithin

YVONNE BROWN

Women of Influence

Affirm & Pursue

I am a Woman of Influence because I help women to soar beyond their past and become the best version of themselves. A Woman of Influence who no longer dwells in past mistakes but aspires to be greater, I lead with a servant's heart and willingly share the wealth of knowledge attained with my village.

As a woman of influence, I teach women to handle their money matters and begin to attain a wealthy mindset so they can live the life they are so deserving of. Queens, it is time to stop dwelling and begin to live, because you deserve to exhale.

Bio:

Yvonne Brown, a native of Philadelphia, Pennsylvania is making her mark as a Women Empowerment Coach. She is driven by her desire to help women to soar beyond their past in order to become the best versions of themselves.

As a project manager for over ten years, Yvonne frequently found herself being a source of support and knowledge for other women in the workplace and other areas of her life. In 2020, she decided to launch a coaching business to be able to fully utilize her gift and to be accessible to even more women. Because positive affirmations played a major role in her personal journey, Yvonne shares messages of empowerment through a t- shirt line (Myndful Tees Boutique) of affirming words encouraging women to believe that they are loved, deserve happiness and are enough.

She also offers courses to support women in reaching their goals through the Affirm & Pursue Academy, focusing on self-love, money matters, and the pursuit of purpose. She is the co-author of two amazing anthology projects: Our Truth Is Not A Lie and The Evolution Effect, and plans to author more books for her audience and create retreats of healing and restoration for women.

Follow this Queen:

FB: https://www.facebook.com/yvonnebrownexhales/

IG: https://www.instagram.com/yvonnebrownexhales/

TENESA MOBLEY

Women of Influence

The Power of YOU

In the midst of a pandemic, Tenesa has coauthored and written her own book, which are both best sellers. She's also started a nonprofit organization in her home state Alabama and Georgia which will give people who've experienced the struggles of life a second chance to become productive citizens.

Bio:

Tenesa Mobley is a 2x bestselling author who's from Greene County, Alabama. She's the proud mother of one son and grandson. She currently resides in North Fulton, Ga.

Follow this Queen:

https://www.Instagram.com/thepowerofyou_tm

ANGELA FOXWORTH

Women of Influence

Author: *The Pain Behind the Smile, Pray, Slay and Collect and Women Win*

I am a Woman of Influence because my platform in life is to see women win!!! I do that by leading by example. I have been able to show through consistency, transparency, and hard work that there is not anything you can't accomplish. And with the belief in yourself that you are unique, you do not have to look or act like anyone else to be a trendsetter and someone to look up to.

Bio:

My name is Angela Foxworth, and at 40 years old I left my career as a financial analyst to pursue my dream of being a talk show host. Now, I am a red-carpet host, the reigning US Majesty Woman 2020, and, most importantly, a best-selling author and a television talk show host! My show is the *Angela Foxworth Show* and my intention is to motivate, educate, and inspire.

Being an author and talk show host allows me to promote positive reinforcement and true change in the community through the purest form of communication there is. I feel blessed and honored to finally be doing what I absolutely have wanted to do my entire life.

Follow this Queen:

https://www.facebook.com/thepainbehindthesmile

https://www.instagram.com/afoxradio

DR. STACY L. HENDERSON

Women of Influence

**Dr. Stacy L. Henderson & Associates Coaching
and Consulting, LLC**

A domestic violence survivor turned advocate, Dr. Henderson has been featured in numerous media outlets, sharing her story of triumph over tragedy. She has worked on projects with several television and cable networks, highlighting the stories of domestic abuse survivors and their healing and recovery journeys - while raising awareness of domestic abuse.

She also worked on Congressional initiatives to get tougher abuse perpetrator laws enforced (President Clinton and President Obama Administrations), and she is active with the National Coalition Against Domestic Violence. She trusts in God and relies on faith-based doctrines, and shares her personal experiences to uplift, motivate, and inspire.

Bio:

Dr. Stacy L. Henderson is a retired Naval Officer with more than 25 years of military experience. She is an International Best-Selling Author, Certified Professional Life Coach and Inspirational Speaker. She has conducted Workshops, Seminars, and Training Evolutions on a global platform, as part of her commitment to helping others achieve their best mental, physical, and spiritual health.

This Proverbs 31 Woman is a devoted Wife, Mother, and Grandmother. To God be the Glory!

Follow This Queen:

https://www.facebook.com/StacyLHenderson

https://www.instagram.com/SLHenderson007

SHERATON GATLIN

Women of Influence

VoirBelle LLC.

As I grew older, I grew wiser. I now realize that everything I went through was on purpose, for a purpose. And not necessarily just for my purpose, but to help inspire and lead someone else to theirs. I chose to use my experiences and lessons learned so others will see and understand that they are not alone, and if I can WIN they can too. You have to trust the process and keep the faith!

Bio:

Sheraton Gatlin is an International Published Celebrity Makeup Artist in the beauty industry and a 4X International Best-Selling Author, as seen on ABC, NBC, CBS, FOX, CW Digital Journal, and Telemundo. Sheraton has worked with notable filmmakers and her work has been published in the American Spa Magazine, Glambitious, In The City Magazine, and the Women of Wealth Magazine.

Sheraton is currently continuing to grow her business and perfecting her craft!

Follow this Queen:

FB: @VoirBelle by Sheraton

IG: @voirbelle

GERVAISE GUYTON

Women of Influence

The Dirty Man: A Memoir of Healing & Deliverance from Sex Abuse

Queen GerVaise provides an environment of healing when she speaks, providing hope and insight that inspires survivors and the non-abused alike to seek healing and wholeness. GerVaise continues to make an immediate impact in the communities in which she serves while on the frontline transforming survivors' lives as a certified hospital advocate and authorized facilitator! Queen GerVaise's drive to eliminate sex abuse from families, communities, and countries is making an impact in our world.

Bio:

GerVaise Sarah Guyton is a public speaker, author, and sex abuse and domestic violence survivor. Over the past 15 years, public audiences and those who learn of the amazing journey of healing and deliverance have persistently asked her to write a book. *The Dirty Man* is the first book in a four-part series that details so many miracles surrounding the residual impacts of childhood sexual abuse and domestic violence. The candid revelatory details of the sexual and domestic violence traumas GerVaise has survived often encourage those who have been abused to disclose their traumas, in some cases for the first time.

Queen GerVaise not only shares her personal experience, but also the entire book is filled with invaluable insights which help victims combat their traumas.

Follow this Queen:

https://www.facebook.com/Queen.GerVaise

https://www.instagram.com/Queen.GerVaise/

DR. JACQUELYN WILSON

Women of Influence

Surprisethestruggling, Book (Noonjewels)

There's nothing more rewarding to me than assisting the woman I once was. The wind beneath my wings is giving back. Teaching what I've learned. Leading the loss broken little girls by awakening within them what they didn't know existed. Creating entrepreneurs. Pulling their purpose out. Granting hope in the midst of struggle.

I took the fruits thrown and created a punch!

Bio:

Dr Jacquelyn Wilson is the CEO of MMOBENT. Executive Director of #Surprisethestruggling Npo. Founder of Thestopbullyingproject & the Dr. Wilson Leadership Academy. Chaplain. Motivational speaker/Clarity Coach. Host of the Grief Circle O & Queens Don't Trip We Adjust Our Crowns movement!

Follow this Queen:

Www.facebook.com/Drwilson @Surprisethestruggling

Www.instagram.com/originalstreetdoctor @Surprisethestruggling

SHELLY LEE

Women of Influence

Pen. Paper. Publish.

I am a Woman of Influence because I seek God for everything. I believe that without God, it cannot be done. I believe that we all can succeed, and I have no problem paying it forward!

Bio:

Shelly Lee is the Owner of Pen. Paper. Publish. She self-published *God Spoke and I Listened* and *The Sheldra Series-An Unknown Love-Book One.* She is currently working on her next 2 books.

In addition to being an author, she is a speaker, ghostwriter, book coach, and proofreader.

Follow this Queen:

https://www.facebook.com/authorshellylee

https://www.instagram.com/ladyleebooks

DR. TERESA WESLEY

Women of Influence

Luke Management, LLC

Dr. Wesley, also known as T.T. McGil and Dr. T, thrives to shine a light on all that she comes in contact with to reiterate that their lives are a gift from God, and that they are here for a purpose – and to use their time wisely. She is the author of self-published *Vision, Faith, and Resilience: Affirmations for Life,* and *Think like a Weight Breaker. Not Like A Weight Taker.* The hope is that all of the eyes that grace those pages of inspiration can enhance their life and fulfill their purpose.

T. T. McGil has authored the *Sparrow Mystery Series,* and her first book *Sparrow: The Water's Edge* is screen ready, and is followed by the soon-to-be-released *Sparrow: The Night Ends.* Both are equipped with a female protagonist that has a strong faith and will fight to the end for truth (book information found on www.TTMcGil.com).

Please see the review for *Sparrow The Night Ends,* for a great read full of mystery and suspense. https://drharinipmurali.wordpress.com/2020/07/23/a-review-of-sparrow-the-night-ends-by-t-t-mcgill/#more-635

Bio:

Dr. Teresa Wesley, MD (pen name T.T. McGil) is a Wife, Mother, Child of God, Chief Medical Officer, Physician Author, Producer, and Motivational Speaker. She has an acumen for leadership and empowerment that is founded on her faith. You can reach Dr. Wesley/TT McGil at www.TTMcGil.com

Follow this Queen:

FB: https://www.facebook.com/TeresaWesley and https://www.facebook.com/TTMcGil

CARMEN RODGERS

Women of Influence

Little Hidden Treasures Learning Center

I am a Woman of Influence because my faith in God is the center of everything; so I CANNOT fail. I lead by example and I am always open to learning from anyone. As a dedicated, hardworking, standup woman, I try to be an inspiration to all women.

I'm kind with a giving heart to anyone in my life, and I've been told that I'm everything any girl, young lady, or woman aims to be in life. I am very far from being perfect, but I'm real.

Bio:

Carmen Rodgers is the owner of Little Hidden Treasures Learning Center. She has been running her childcare center for the past 6 years while also having a full-time career (23 years) as a police detective.

Follow this Queen:

https://www.facebook.com/Little-Hidden-Treasures-Learning-Center-930544850313573/

QUEEN, ARE YOU READY TO PLAY YOUR ROYAL POSITION?!

Join Our Women Win TRIBE NOW!

APPLY FOR YOUR EPIC OPPORTUNITY TO JOIN OUR FUTURE INTERNATIONAL BEST-SELLING QUEEN COLLABORATIVE BOOK, SHARE YOUR MESSAGE ON OUR GLOBAL STAGE, AND BUILD A REAL SISTERHOOD WITH STORNG WOMEN OF FAITH!

APPLY NOW: http://bit.ly/38FFXjY

Or

TEXT: tribe to 470.730.7424

Or

Email Us: info@jesuscoffeeandprayer.com

Subject Line: Join the Tribe!

Made in the USA
Columbia, SC
01 May 2021